STRANGE PIETÀ

D1564894

S T R A N G E   P I E T À

gregory fraser

Introduction by Robert Fink

Texas Tech University Press

This book is typeset in Optima. The paper used in this book
meets the minimum requirements of ANSI/NISO Z39.48-
1992 (R1997). ♾

Designed by Brendan Liddick

Printed in the United States of America

Library of Congress Cataloging-in-Publication Data
Fraser, Gregory.
   Strange pietà / Gregory Fraser.
      p.   cm. — (Walt McDonald first-book poetry series)
   ISBN 0-89672-500-6 (cloth : alk. paper)
   ISBN 0-89672-544-8 (paper : alk. paper)
   1. Spina bifida—Patients—Poetry. 2. Brothers—Poetry.
I. Title. II. Series.

PS3606.R423 S77 2003
813'.6—dc21

                                        2002156607

05 06 07 08 09 10 11 12 / 9 8 7 6 5 4 3

Texas Tech University Press
Box 41037
Lubbock, Texas 79409-1037 USA
800.832.4042
www.ttup.ttu.edu

This book is dedicated to Jonathan Scott Fraser

ACKNOWLEDGMENTS

Grateful acknowledgment is made to the following publications in which some of these poems first appeared, sometimes in different versions:

Georgetown Review: "Losing Father's Pocketwatch"
Gulf Coast: "A Friend's Divorce" and "Glass"
Paris Review: "Still Life"
Puerto del Sol: "Coward"
Riversedge: "The Sign"
Southern Review: "Cruiser," "End of Days," "Rejoice," "Strange Pietà," and "Work"
Texas Review: "Down Time"
Western Humanities Review: "Ars Poetica," "Blood Work," and "How It Happened"

I wish to thank the following mentors and editors for their guidance and support: Michael Griffith, Daniel Halpern, Edward Hirsch, Richard Howard, Cynthia Macdonald, the late William Matthews, James Olney, Robert Phillips, and Adam Zagajewski.

Thanks to the Associated Writing Programs, the Cultural Arts Council of Houston/Harris County, Inprint, Inc., Teachers & Writers Collaborative, my former students and colleagues at Wittenberg University and St. John's University, and the writing programs at Columbia University and the University of Houston. Special thanks to Robert Fink and the Texas Tech University Press.

I am grateful for the continued encouragement of my family and friends. I am especially indebted to Nancy Ford, Darlene Gold, Seth Hurwitz, Dave Johnson, Doug Larsen, and Pimone Triplett. My deepest gratitude goes to my parents and to Susannah Mintz.

CONTENTS

INTRODUCTION

In the title poem of Andrew Hudgins's *Saints & Strangers,* Elizabeth Marie, the poem sequence's persona, receives the following epiphany: "One glory of a family is / you'd never choose your kin." She can now affirm that when you learn to accept the strangeness of your family, you "get to be, / in turn, someone you'd never choose to be." The key word in these lines is *glory:* the glory of a family is both its saintliness and its strangeness, and even though her life has been one trial after another, Elizabeth Marie celebrates, in hindsight, her *getting to be* chosen rather than having the opportunity to choose.

Gregory Fraser, in his poetry collection *Strange Pietà,* also celebrates the strangeness of a family engaged in "the beauty of repair, / with its stunning frailties, dazzling displays of risk and grace" (part 7 of "Strange Pietà"). This family has learned that our lives become meaningful when we can "glorify / our fruitless efforts and fallings short" ("Rejoice"). They now can rejoice "that every sacrifice demands / an elevation, that each cruel twist (of knife, fate, wrist) vouches for / one good turn" ("Rejoice"). This family's "cruel twist" is the youngest son, Jonathan, who has come "into the world disfigured, into the fold of history / and circumstance to bleat with the rest of us / brave sheep, cowardly lions" (part 8 of "Strange Pietà).

It is Jonathan who has inspired his brother, the book's poet-persona, to write this "Song of My Other" (part 8 of "Strange Pietà"), the poet declaring in the opening section, "I am here to speak for a grown man / of thirty-three (a grown man so to speak). . . . " Jonathan is the *word*—"subject of a long, complex construction" which Jonathan's mother, "in the silent agonies of composition, never could / perfect" ("Ars Poetica"); so, as the opening poem "Ars Poetica," declares, it is now the poet's turn to attempt perfecting his brother, and his family, by means of the poet's art—a cold light focused on the poet himself, on his mother Barbara, his father David, his brother Tom, and especially on Jonathan, born with spina bifida, a subject inspiring no beatific light, no beauty, nothing less than a truth that sheds no meaning but the reality that "human can mean this"—"a spinal tap at two, feasting / through a tube, a rite of passage a needle in the arm / three times a day." And worse. Much worse.

The poet's art will not make light of Jonathan, nor of his family. This art will not be pretty; neither will it be a composition of despair. *Strange Pietà* is a study of the heroic, the "limits of the flesh"—a "brother's teeth, / tombstones in his gums' soft clay, jutting everywhere / and gray, his tongue that tangles on 'Hello'" ("Ars Poetica"). It is a book paying "homage" to "parents' names, / signed in black on a stack of forms, admitting failure, doubt, fear," a book about a family at worship—their daily devotion to the flaws, the faults that give heft and form to the void of easy, abstract beauty—"Light's been made too long of my brother's state" ("Ars Poetica").

Strange Pietà defines "what being tested means" ("Ars Poetica"). In doing so, the poet not only defines Jonathan and his family, but defines us as well if we have learned not to pretend that life is "brighter than it is," if we can sing the song of ourselves "without mincing words," if we can affirm with the poet that "the world's an ugly baby," but a "baby we must love" ("Ars Poetica").

With a title like *Strange Pietà,* the book prepares us to expect Biblical allusions, especially to Mary the mother of Jesus, cradling her crucified son. Jonathan *is* thirty-three, the traditional age of Jesus when he was crucified, and in most ways Jonathan *is* dead to the poet, Jonathan usually not even recognizing his brother; but Jonathan is alive, resurrected from a residential care facility to live in an apartment of his own, hold down a job stuffing envelopes, packing shoeshine kits, "counting out wing nuts" ("Down Time"). And the poet *is* on a religious pilgrimage of sorts to confess his fear, his guilt and shame at living a life apart from his brother but not apart from the consequences of having Jonathan as a brother.

In Section I of the book, the poet seems to be invoking his Muses (Jonathan, his mother, and his father), while also introducing the poet's conflict—his need to confess what he perceives as his sin of being *other* than his brother Jonathan, and seek some means of expiation, some form of grace. The poet acknowledges that he is speaking for each member of his family, but as brother to Jonathan, the poet needs to identify principally with his brother, his "other": "This time, I follow too, working backwards / from the periods of his pupils, joining the sentence fragments / and stunted syllables making up his recollections" ("Down Time"). The poet, however, admits that his "need to make perfect, / improve on my brother's efforts, is just another form of afflic-tion" ("Down Time").

In "Ignis Fatuus," the poet addresses his mother: "Forgive me, mother, for I have sinned. This is my first confession." His process of expiation will lead him by means of his poetic pilgrimage "to suture, with ink-black thread, / the gash between split sons." This perceived split is what leads the poet to attempt a psychological return to the womb, to become his brother, be born again as Jonathan, to know Jonathan, and in doing so, know himself. He calls to his mother for salvation for himself and for Jonathan, seeking a new begin-ning: "Mother, / draw us to your breast. Suckle a new nativity. Teach us to breathe."

In "Lemon," as he does at the conclusion of each of the three main sec-tions, the poet ends with hope, affirming that the miracle of the mundane can lead to grace, a respite from the reality of an unfair world. In this poem, the *miracle* is, as the title states, a lemon—both sour and brilliantly, beautifully yellow, symbol of hope and mystery, a sign against despair. After months of "crying out without crying out," after the poet's trying to breathe, gasping for breath, a serendipity occurs: "yesterday on the dingy / pavement, below one scuff of cloud, a brilliant, unbruised lemon / rolled past my feet like a drop of sun, fiery slaver." The poet draws a new breath, his mouth exploding with "*lemon, lemon.*"

Section II maintains the tone of self-examination, the process of expiation, while also being fire and ice, a study of passion and fury, of loss, failed rela-tionships, the tension between men and women, between a father and his son. This section focuses more on the poet than on his family. He looks to his past to examine his lost life, his guilt, and he admits he is uncertain about so much, often feeling like more of an "eavesdropper" listening to the grief of others, unable to take action, comfort "those in anguish" ("Coward"). When he tries to offer "consolation" to his friend after learning of the friend's recent divorce, the poet can only mutter "something about trust / that sounded like I knew" ("A Friend's Divorce"). Then, as in "Lemon," the spiritual comes as a surprise, rising from the mundane—brown garbage bags "stuffed with yard work," against the curb, like "monks in cassocks / huddled to pay devotion in the dark, backlit by grace" ("A Friend's Divorce").

Past memories of real and imagined loves lead the poet to admit his inabil-ity "to face beauty head on, to hear its harsh appraisal," but still he can dream up a high school past in which a "glorious present would come alive, inhaling the future, exhaling the past, / while keeping them invisible to us as summer breath" ("Cruiser"). In this past, the poet's days "were not a series yet / of might-as-wells & might-have-beens," not yet the present that leads the poet to assert that we must forgive because we can, "because we're all alone in this / together, every crime is ours, & not to forgive is the worst / we can commit" ("Cruiser").

Section II also looks to the poet's imagined future, his ultimately becoming like his brother Jonathan has always been—defined by "gibberish and drool" ("Still Life"), but the poet can affirm that although this life is often "blinding void," it also offers us the surprise of "rapture" ("Still Life").

Ours is a world of sweets and sours, more often being the sours of decrepitude, war, death; so the poet calls for a poem by a friend "devoted to the damaged, lost, and pilfered goods" ("How To Begin A Poetry Reading"). The poet looks to work for a kind of salvation, the work his ghost father is doing in the poem "Work," kneeling, "worshiping again / in the only church he ever trusted"—the earth, specifically the rock garden he and his son planted when the poet was a boy. He joins his father's ghost in this work: "My father and I are sharing our love / of privacy together," leading the poet to Praise. He sings praise to the cardinal sweeping "down from the sky / to show off his crimson miter." "Praise to grass / for getting stomped on day after day, / and never once complaining" ("Work").

In "Rejoice," the final poem of Section II, the poet continues his theme of praise in spite of all the reasons not to. He declares, "Let's pay / due homage to our griefs for what they are: gifts that keep on giving / off their opposites, in perfect inverse degrees." He can now "confess: who really places / faith in a realm apart from ruin." He also calls on us to confess: "For once, let's not evade: we are / lonely, every one of us, and frightened, those who deny / it, most of all." His conclusion, therefore, is that we should praise this fallen world, this life of almost constant complications: "Then let's praise again, as from the start, that everything / is anything / but simple" ("Rejoice").

The third and final section of *Strange Pietà*, making up almost a third of the book, is the title poem in ten parts celebrating the poet's family, developing the poet's analysis of how being the brother of Jonathan, the son of Barbara and David, has affected the poet, how being a member of this family has taught him to acknowledge beauty as "that which can't be borrowed / or sought, which must be fallen into during carefree / exercise" (part 4). And there isn't much that is carefree for this family: "Worry, for my family, is a form of prayer," with *luck* meaning "redemption through suffering and love" (part 2). The miracles in their lives *are* their lives (part 1). In this strange pietà,

Jonathan is the risen, ironic savior of his family, proclaiming his "slurred sermon" to his brother, admonishing him to "Prize / the world's caprice, . . . worship / that. We must learn to cherish chance to have one" (part 8).

There is much to discover in this poem, set literally and symbolically on the Fourth of July, a family celebration of personal independence, a declaration against fear and grief and guilt, an affirmation of all members of the family. This affirmation has not come easily, as the flashbacks to a painful past confirm: A mother's having to face the reality of a son with spina bifida, her struggling against depression, her face "that of a china plate / shattered inside a U-Haul box and epoxied back / together" (part 8), shouting her "bellow" at the world—"a sound whose waves ripple still" (part 3). A father surviving "his own difficult / labor—the painful, drawn-out delivery of explanation" (part 3), racing to the telephone, "gently lifting the handset, / . . . swaddling the ugly / facts in apothegms and whispers" (part 3). Two brothers isolated from their mother, having to "study" her "through a door three-quarters shut, guarded / by paternal rule forbidding access" (part 3), "one of those silences you never stop hearing" (part 3). A youngest brother who at the Fourth of July family celebration spews "corn on the cob like confetti in parades," soils Depends, slurps and burps Sprite, slobbers (part 4). Theirs is a family for whom "normal" has come to mean shame (part 2).

At the close of this day, the "family is gathered under families of stars, / ungraspable sparklers" as they watch the Fourth of July fireworks bursting over "the lower constellations of the city, / every one of us . . . oohing and aahing" (part 10). The poet can now celebrate what his brother Jonathan has taught the family: "To honor / Something deeply . . . / is to love what's hapless, vulnerable" (part 8). This is the promise of salvation for the poet and his family; this is the promise of Jonathan.

one

ARS POETICA

for Jonathan

All poetry begins, from now on, with my brother's legs.
Think how once he ranged, shod in blood, the world

our mother fashioned, deep within the smithy of herself,
that inverse globe she shaped, its four corners and three seasons,

clock how fast he raced, by the light of his becoming,
kicking up the dust of the broken egg, into the fields

of genes, the Highlands of our father's clan, south
to Tuscany, at speeds beyond mere verb, velocities no

mind could read, for that was the body's language, cells
in a freeplay of compounding, the run-on sentence of the flesh,

until the dark germ rode, dormant fate for steed, along
my brother's spine, flung the false logic of his DNA, dragged

him down. In the beginning there was the word, and my brother
was that word, the subject of a long, complex construction

our mother, in quiet agonies of composition, never could
perfect. She let her old art die, as others will, who'll write no more

3

of dawn, the daily labors of the sun (as if they might espy
in nature something of their own) to crawl out from under

this floating rock, knock the night back whence it came,
break the bars of longitude and latitude, ozone and cloud,

to flush the cheek. Making light is easy. Watch:
half-wit, numbskull, saphead, lamebrain, nincompoop, dope.

Light's been made too long of my brother's state. X it
from all songs. Its images and metaphors are moot.

Banish them to the inky mote from which they sprang,
the period that closed the final chapter of the world

before this one we animate. Wave farewell to verse
that rollicks by light's name. It cannot ease the loads

our hearts must ferry through this life. House a proper
darkness in your lines. This is homage to my parents' names,

signed in black on a stack of forms, admitting failure, doubt,
fear, and my brother to a hospice hours from home.

Goodbye to light to the highest power, goodbye. Once,
it was claimed some rapture pure and warm

knelt down in your blood while you called on grace
to free you from the confines of your clay.

Poems must reflect that light, respond in kind, you say.
Too bad. All missives marked for God are now dismissed.

Mail no more numbered letters on the air, posted high
on your suspension of disbelief. The limits of the flesh

are my brother's knees where his thighs
should be, and Grace is the name of the nurse

4

who took my brother's matter in her hands, cleansed the marks
of birth with alcohol (unholy water, that), raised him

to the shocking air, stares of his deliverers at the miracle
gone wrong. Our God is far away, a lousy correspondent,

and that brings pain. But measure the distances in that ward,
though no one moved. Ponder the gap in my brother's back,

the window to the spine someone forgot to shut,
letting in the draft that froze his fetal growth. From here on,

call God "cause" and be done with it, sorting out effects:
a boy who'll never stroll, dance, skip, leap, land.

Mull over this: when lightning bugs have forged a sky
of the back yard, prompting the image on a pad,

my brother could not catch one star,
or make himself a cosmos in a jar.

Let's set aside the pad, and while we're at it
hush the mating calls of rhyme. Too loud a music harms

my brother's ears. That last end rhyme was precisely that.
Drink to its long reign. The couplet is no hero. Better

face that fact, as well, no matter how good looking,
smart or strong. It cannot stride on shining feet,

scale tower walls, unlock my brother's mind
from its dark jail. Heroic is a spinal tap at two, feasting

through a tube, a rite of passage a needle in the arm
three times a day, questing clues from the hamartia

of his cells. That's what being tested means. Suppose
we make verse blank, to match my brother's eyes.

No—simply watch him turn them outside in,
bound to a wheelchair in his room, and not say for once

he looks "at peace." So saying, aren't we throwing
lifelines to ourselves, drowning in the fact that human

can mean this? Douse the light of meaning, too,
knowledge, reason, truth. Socrates, before he drank

himself to death, claimed knowing you know nothing
is the crucial thing to know. He said that, knowing nothing

about not knowing. No dialogue can speak without a ring
of sham to my brother's absent mind. Neither can the light

of beauty shed any light on him. Bid it fond adieu.
What have we to lose? Who doesn't know by now

it fills a void until some flaw shows up to make it real?
Worship faults for that. Praise my brother's teeth,

tombstones in his gums' soft clay, jutting everywhere
and gray, his tongue that tangles on "Hello."

Best to shift the poetic terms to these: *slobber,*
blunder, slip. The art of poetry is the art of slur.

That's all ye need to know, plus this:
the world's an ugly baby we must love, sing to

without mincing words. Don't let beauty promise
foolish answers to my brother's drool. Hear his broken

speech when you enjamb. Make your lines as short
as his attention span, long as he can take to request

a Coke. Try: "It's gray today, the earth about
to wet itself again." Good. Now conjure my brother

at thirty-three, soaked to the skin in bed, or celebrating
birthday dinner at Chuck E. Cheese, playing

with his model trains, the work that is his play.
See him on the real job now, mainstreamed in a factory,

a streak of urine forking down his leg. Go from there
and bear in mind what poor Keats coughed

about the ore in every line. Just swap the ore
for cordovan, black, and brown, brush and chamois cloth—

the kit my brother assembles for fifty cents an hour.
Depict as best you can the negative capabilities

of his fingers, as the foreman hears another tin of Kiwi
hit the floor. Write long into the night, until your right hand

cramps like his. If you're left-handed, switch.
Come morning, strike every line that cannot warrant

the loss of patience with the value of a dime, which my brother
cannot count. Choose that labor for your theme.

If not, prepare to be crossed out, like a number in subtraction,
the simple math my brother fails to grasp, the number

that you are. In honor of his bones, distort reality
as you please. All verse forms are now deformed.

As for the lights left on, you know what's required:
snuff the light of passion, and its parent, fire.

My brother will never know the conflagration
of a lover's kiss, or how to treat his body to itself

in the private dark. Gone the highlights
of the sporting life, to boot. Touchdowns,

backhands, fast-break hoops cinching the game
have no place in poems any more. This life is not

a "crack of light." Despite Nabokov's phrase,
it's a compromise between two darks, the place

where birth and death meet each other halfway
for a time. Don't pretend it's brighter than it is.

Take your cues from my brother's hair, hectic black.
Enough to focus elsewhere, at least for now,

delving into doom for its own sake.
Remember: this is only the beginning.

DOWN TIME

Over Sunday supper, lasagna and garlic bread, my brother tells us
(with some heavy prompting) what work is like, how it feels to make
a buck, which is double his hourly wage. He spills out a roll call
of fellow workers—Colby, Simon, Dwayne, his best friend, Shawn—
a dozen men hunched around a table, stuffing envelopes, packing
shoe-shine kits, counting out wing nuts, then ziplocking ten in a bag.

My mother passes the salad, father the wine, while I elicit stammers
about a motley crew: the salvage of auto wrecks, Huntington's,
Down's Syndrome, hunkering down to business, concentrating
on the task at hand, each of their faces soon a sweatshop in itself.
(Lemons, Plato would have deemed them, had he written
in our republic.) It isn't long, though—never is—before

my brother's thoughts grow cluttered with sudden
absences, random erasures, and the dim recesses of his mind
become his mind again, words trailing off, eyes wandering
aimlessly after them. This time, I follow too, working backwards
from the periods of his pupils, joining the sentence fragments
and stunted syllables making up his recollections. I wake

in his Craftmatic bed, feel the live-in aide shake one shoulder
to rouse him. I am there when she hoists both arms and pulls
a sweater tightly down, until his head passes safely through
the birth canal of the turtleneck. At the shop all day
I hover beside him—the Virgil in me longing to offer advice,
a helping hand, but somehow I sense my need to make perfect,

improve on my brother's efforts, is just another form of affliction.
A bolt flies from his fingers, rattles on cold concrete, sour notes
my brother doesn't hear, and I wonder how many times, down
on two good knees, someone in this nation of endless goods
has slammed a fist against the floor and railed
when the bag of parts for a child's first two-wheeler,

a new bookcase for the den, lacks a vital lock-washer,
nut or screw. How many have leaped to feet that won't
fail them, now and maybe never, dialed a toll-free number,
vented their healthy spleens on some claims-department clerk?
I have, and I have had to learn to swallow that frustration
for the castor oil it is. No machine's at fault:

my brother's defects deserve the blame, and I am here
to vouch for them, for his damaged goods that cannot be
returned, no matter which receipt was saved—afterbirth
or ward's delivery bill. I'm here to speak for a grown man
of thirty-three, a grown man so to speak, rolling back his chair,
his four-wheeler, at the close of the day, and spotting the bolt

that left a hole in another's life, disabled some best-laid plans.
Won't he look down on himself who can't stand up, bend over
to retrieve the errant steel? Don't get me wrong. I'm not sure
if any one man's suffering should be doled out for all to taste.
Yet I feel obliged to raise a voice for working stiffs,
when these are my brother's index fingers, pinkies, thumbs.

A year ago, after state funds hit a drought, but the men
still had to report for work, my brother kissed Shawn
on the mouth, then groped his crotch. I can't tell you how
often I've envisioned my brother's hands, the bad one
and the worse, parked on that workshop bench, idling
like a pair of eighteen-wheelers in a truck-stop lot, waiting

for industry to lurch into gear again, then moving
down, at last, to his own lap—the edge of action.
Or how frequently I've eavesdropped on his dream
of desire, his thirst to give and receive just one caress
without pity in it, for one hand through his hair
not serving as a comb, one to hold, not for balance

in the tub, or support while some injection needles in.
I've tried my best to imagine what it must be like for him
never to have sipped from a lover's cup,
or suffered the hangover after lust's intoxications.
And I have questioned whether any theft is more forgivable
than a stolen kiss, if any move toward intimacy is false.

They suspended my brother for thirty days,
made him humble himself before Shawn, learn that form
of compensation. Do you suppose his apology came across
like most (I bet it did) in a muffled voice, as if spoken
from behind a closet door? I'll wager even he knows
it's best for shame to leave the self through cracks and keyholes.

Now a shadow falls across my brother's face
from somewhere behind it, a glimmer perhaps
of remembrance—the forced labor of patience,
the hours losing their perfect roundness, stretching into
encephalitic shapes, the clock another cripple
in the room. He seems about to speak, then utters

nothing, letting vacancy talk for him.
It's getting late. My mother's up to her elbows
in soapsuds and pots, and dad has wheeled
his third and final son into the den. They'll sing
along for half an hour to Kenny Rogers,
then drive the few hushed miles

to the small apartment my brother shares
with another ward of the state. Maybe tonight
I'll tag along, tuck him into bed, not leave it
for someone who gets paid to. Perhaps
I'll kiss my brother good night, wish him
a productive week, full of pleasurable occupations.

IGNIS FATUUS

1.

In August swelter, fourth-month scorch,
while rising and setting suns
blistered on cross horizons, and lemonade
pitchers popped with sweat
under harsh interrogation lamps of noon,
while limp tomato plants singed at the stake,
no gust billowed the sky's dead sail,
and blue jays flickered like hotter,
robins and cardinals like cooler, flames,
while pick-up stickball games, creek
beds, thick-furred family dogs on stoops
swooned backwards with heat
exhaustion, fevered strokes,

your mother couldn't wait
another hour in the scalding nineties
(her lined brow strung with worry
beads, hands wrung raw as nerves)
yet somehow waited another day
brushing triple digits, one more
third-degree burn of a week,
for that first soft tap on the inside
of her womb's self-locking door—
the gentle rap of knuckles not quite
knuckles, from her latest boarder,

on three-term lease, paying rent
in small installments of his girth.

No knock came.
Instead, a hot flash burst out of some
frayed vein, some fritz in her body electric,
and climbed—an inverse lightning—
from swollen feet to knees, bloated
waist to chest, floor by occupied floor
to atticked brain, until all she could see
was your brother, trapped in a crib
of ribs, wrapped in a flammable
quilt of her flesh's knitting, unable
to wrest himself free, cry out
wordlessly in pain, breathe
any more of their shared blood.

While parked cars rocked at tarry
moorings, black squirrels barked
like hellhounds, maples turned up
palms for alms of rain, and not
a bobby-socked girl, in sidewalk
play, cracked a maternal back,
your mother couldn't stop
the sirens' shrieking (sonic flares
all day in her third ear), crazed lights
from running wild through sleepless nights,
or your brother from being
torched alive, many times,
though still unborn. . . .

2.

Forgive me, mother, for I have sinned.
This is my first confession. I have
clutched, like treasured heirlooms,
these awful conceptions of yours,
passed down sure as genes,

14

clung to them in place of him,
embraced chimeric flames and not
the man, twisted in their image,
forged in pieces whole. I have
listened to your conjured blaze,
its smoke-tipped tongues a fiery
Babel calling my brother back
to his pre-birth, incomprehensible

part by part. I have followed
in your footsteps skirting the strange,
mismade, and jerked away
quickly from touch, like the hand
of a child from tempting fire,
the curious toddler your one boy
couldn't become. Like you,
I've spied through glass
the cooed-to infants' wriggles,
been deafened by soft rubbings
(pink and powder blue)
against sealed skin. Premature
Cassandra at twenty-nine,

you foresaw mocking staggers,
pratfalls on recess fields, foreheard
"retard," "dunce," jeers I might be
bruised by in his stead, archive
in a well-wired head. Now I'm left
to suture, with ink-black thread,
the gash between split sons, stitch space
you opened so I might breathe.
This may explain our gaps in speech
when you sometimes phone, attention
veering in conversation, and must be why
I opted above for "your," the pronoun
at one remove from the genuine.

Forgive me, mom: it's been a stanza
since I last confessed, a formless,
foreshortened sonnet of nights
since last I stepped outside
my body into yours, drawn
by the ignis fatuus
glowing in your equidistance, lit
within you still. I know taboo,
that mothers are for exiting only.
Yet I have little choice except
re-entry, small solace but attempts
to dip in your fool's fire, cleanse
these marks of the abled:

a straight-toothed smile, nimble
toes, two located hips. You taught me
to survive by mimicking loss,
meeting it face to face with the same
blank stare. So in his absence
I became my brother's ghost
(though in reverse, passing visibly
through lucid walls). Tonight,
I must erase these muscled thighs,
digits adept at plucking riffs
from steel, and be reduced
to the cinder I am
compared to him.

3.

It's three A.M. Soon, I will drift
into something like sleep, and waken
backwards at three A.M., believing
I have pried myself from time,
that three-mouthed hound of present,
past and future, fighting itself for my scrap
of meat. Within the hour, I'll be crossing
the thirty deserts of thirty summers

to my brother's botched beginnings,
glinting far ahead: a mirrored SOS
on the blurry threshold of your spirit,
mother, and flesh. Isn't this his standing
signal for me to shamble forward,

not just barefoot, but as a true penitent,
no false sufferer, carrying my feet
at my sides like bloody shoes?
Isn't this his way of prodding me,
in the private code of our most ancient
of fraternal orders, to detach
my movable legs, prop them
under arms and gimp along?
If I am ever to know a heart
light enough to carry like a tune,
ever to distill potential into one true act,
speak sincerely beyond my mother,
with my brother, tongue,

I must hobble on such makeshift
crutches, while lymph nodes callus
and twin black nests of hair chafe off.
May I lurch across these molten sands,
until a halo flares above my head,
one ring the untamed sun will tiger
through, gnash me open at the shuntless
neck, drape a cape of red
down a sweat-ridged back. Then,
when the white bull stirs, lowers
its bleached skull to charge, let me whip
this cape to save the skin I'll later pitch
beneath stars glistening like drops of fat.

Holy Barbara, mother of God,
now is the hour of our return, like culprits,
to the scene of your primal crime,
with its lack of culprits, glut of victims,

statute of endless limitations. Smaller
and smaller we'll grow from current
sight, closer and closer with distance
covered (almost infinite, like tracks of trains,
with our regression), until we slip inside
the cross-shaped wound, as yet unhealed,
above your breasts—the fissure opened
when you tore the Son of Sons from around
your neck, cast him into doubt's dark pit.

4.

Terrible is the light within the house
of flesh, terrible the heat, both of them
seeming to stream from our fused brain,
a miner's beam. We must roll up,
like a sleeve, our strong right arm,
thrust the stark bone in, grasp
our brother by the natal tail, pull
ourselves where we belong:
deeper inside. Together, we must burn
as he once did in you, for you, must
skirl like him upstairs, swaddled
in fire. Only then can he rise
again, be reborn before born,

rub the sleep from dormant coals.
Only then rush to our aid
(uncomely hero, unlikely savior)
sliding in urgent spirals down
your windpipe's pole. Mother, dilate
your eyes. If you can see him
I can see him, pulling on the gloves
of hands no longer welded
to inaction, leaping behind
an engine's outsized wheel,
not pausing for an instant to adjust
his epiblastic helmet, tie saphenous
laces dangling from bootless feet.

Spread them wider
so he can spray with umbilical
hose, fan flames with cooling
sweeps of unbroken water, scale
a hook and ladder of columned bone.
Our son will clamber headlong
toward shattered windows,
unfazed by jagged cascades
slashing open translucent cheeks,
lidless eyes. Once we're fully his,
he will be fully ours
to watch descend
from the second storey,

to cheers of an awe-filled crowd—
ours to witness standing
on two firm stumps, unraveling
himself from thick blankets
of smoke. Look: he's handing
over the unharmed child,
many times his size and age,
whose life he's risked his own
to save, the wailing newborn
who will answer to our names.
Mother, draw us to your breast.
Suckle a new nativity.
Teach us to breathe.

L E M O N

For months without crying out I'd been crying out, like a disconnected
phone in a vacant apartment, an iced red snapper in the fish-shop window,

a pizza dough punched in the solar plexus. I'd been gasping for breath
beneath my ostensible breath, unable to stop from seeing the full moon

as the rolled-back eye of a sleepwalking, cyclopic world,
to locate pain or pleasure, repair or damage, in the opening at dawn,

closing at dusk, of the horizon's wound. But yesterday on the dingy
pavement, below one scuff of cloud, a brilliant, unbruised lemon

rolled past my feet like a drop of sun, fiery slaver . . .
For months I'd been thinking exodus the one true genesis,

torture the only tutor worth the exorbitant fee. I'd concluded
we are little more than footnotes placed by stars

beneath the asterisks of stars, that whatever sense
of a timeless home we might possess was quaint *hommage.*

It must have fallen off the sidewalk display
of the fruit stand on the corner, though of course no fruit stand stood

anywhere in sight. I'd been feeling bitter—over what
it's hard precisely to say: that mustard-stained hot dog wrapper

wrestling wind down the block? My foiled attempts to find,
if not unravel, the seam between the visible and vision?

It blazed across my path—a gilded interjection—then vanished
into the damned and steaming gutter. There isn't much else to tell.

I'd been crying out without crying out for months,
then my mouth exploded with *lemon, lemon* . . .

two

C O W A R D

There's a coward in every eavesdropper. I never realized that
        until one summer night
the trucker who lived next door steered his rig up the gravel drive—
        home from the long haul
to work over his wife. Through the hum of the window fan,
        I heard a crash of glass,
the splintered sound of a busted chair, and lay in bed alone,
        praying it would stop,
listening to her body being thrown against hard luck.
        I knew that doing nothing
is always doing something, and that nothing in this case
        was something hurtful
to a woman getting her share just then. I reached for the bedstand phone.
        What I didn't know was this:
that nothing was going to make it stop, that in a minute I'd be
        setting the receiver back
undialed, telling the part of myself that suddenly needed to hear it
        how I should mind my own
business, it wasn't my fault—there were hotlines, shelters,
        she should call, leave
the monster. Trying not to listen (rips of cloth,
        a muffled cry) yet
straining still to hear, I began to wonder what could lead a man
        to this, a road paved
with what? The constant smack of bugs on windshield glass,
        dead without knowing

what hit them, the air just stopping short? The double yellow line
        at night, blurred to a single
stream, like a piss held in painfully then suddenly let loose
        in Tulsa or Des Moines?
Or the grind of the same twelve gears, up and down, over and over,
        a form of butchery in itself?
Some dishes broke and I couldn't take it any more, pulled
        a pillow over my head.
Hemorrhoids? Back trouble? The threat of jackknifing
        in the rain? After,
I thought I heard her on the stoop, mumbling words of—
        could it possibly
have been shame? It sounded like shame, but now I know
        that was only me throwing
my voice. Next morning, the rig was gone, out on the turnpike,
        its chrome front end beating
down the distance, knocking the wind out of the nation again.
        My neighbor stood on her porch,
studying the hedges, gemmed with dew, between our lots.
        I opened the door, bent
for the newspaper, glanced her way. Her face was a map
        he'd drawn to guide him back
to the crappy little town inside himself, that hellhole without a sheriff
        or a name. Population: one,
or zero, hard to say. She looked at me and smiled—the kind
        of polite smile that,
instead of opening a bridge, holds up a sign that reads, in essence,
        Closed for Repairs.
The hollows of her eyes told me that of all the things
        he'd beaten out of her
it was the hope that things might change that hurt the worst.
        I wanted to show compassion,
say something kind, prove all men weren't scum. That was before
        I'd learned how worthless
consolation is, comforting those in anguish less
        than those at an awkward loss
for any truly helpful words. A school bus rumbled past,
        screeched to a halt

at the end of the block, inhaled some kids. I watched
    until it pulled away,
making sure the driver took the corner wide enough,
    missed the curb.

A FRIEND'S DIVORCE

It was good manners, I suppose, that made him wait
until the meal had ended (napkins set aside, steak bones
in the shallow graves of our empty plates) to tell us

it was final, that the settlement, like a lightning bolt,
had split the house straight down the center, half for her,
half for him: he'd put it on the market in the spring.

We sat awhile not knowing what to say, breaking
the stale bread of silence together. Then my girlfriend called
his wife a lying bitch, and I mumbled something about trust

that sounded like I knew. He raised his glass, nodded
that we were right, but mostly out of kindness for us,
I think, a couple who needed to be right just then

about what keeps two people from falling apart.
It's midnight now, and I can't stop gazing
out the window by my desk. Slats of light are falling

through a gaping hole in the late-October sky, falling
on my friend's front porch like stacks of shirts
and bed sheets from Kopek's Linen Service—

on the two white birches on his well-groomed lawn,
gleaming like the stockings of the prostitute
he brought home one evening for the entire block to see

while his wife was away "on business" in Detroit.
The woman spent the night, but they never went upstairs,
just talked until the pink bruise of dawn appeared,

two old soldiers swapping stories, comparing wounds.
She told him pain could sometimes be a gift,
but that wasn't why most people found it better to give

than to receive—something along those lines,
though it's been months since I learned the details,
and it could be I'm just filling in her words

because I want some larger part in my friend's repair,
because I envy what she, a stranger, could offer him:
the soothing distance I could not. Envy, yes—

so I'm no saint. Neither's he. Still, watching
moonlight glaze the brown garbage bags,
stuffed with yard work, against his curb,

all I can see are monks in cassocks, huddled to pay
devotion in the dark, backlit by grace. I don't know,
maybe that's how I say my prayers these days,

the imagination picking up where the Catholic left off
years ago. Anyway, he was good enough to wash
the dishes afterwards, even scrubbed the blackened grill.

It took him twenty minutes with a Brillo pad,
while my girlfriend and I polished off the cabernet, staring
the candles down. Their flames swayed like two lovers

I'd once seen at the end of a wedding reception, one on either
side of the empty dance floor while the band wound down.
It was clear they'd had a spat, a little too much to drink.

That's why they were slow-dancing with themselves,
each too angry at the other to move toward the center,
each too proud to make the first move to leave.

CRUISER

We would quicken in the vinyl
(velour if we were lucky) of our third mothers,
with their huge eight-chambered hearts & cleavage

deep to the very block, with their buxom dashboards
perfumed with specious pine, their dials & meters, dual bands
& songs for names—*Delta, Regal, Skylark,*

not Vera or Constance or Jane—with their ample
headroom & sturdy bodies forged from ribs, bituminous & ferric,
torn from our state's west side. Think dead

of July of pumping gas by day, Crusoe of the concrete isles,
tending my private garden of stains
that bloomed in rainbow colors after sun- or thundershowers,

dreaming all the asphalt hours of Friday
night with Janet Moscowitz or Ellyn Chanin, Cindy Patterson
or Lisa Koss (I have to strap myself to the pencil's mast

even now to print those names), with Carol Elliot & her flawless mouth
no longer full of correction & lisps. Serve time
in Exxon exile, with customers who sparsely tipped, crowning yourself

the lord & master, nonetheless, of cowering dipsticks,
bold suppressor of steamy uprisings, cleanser of the sins of robin redbreasts,
crows, the Great Emancipator of genie-like fumes. Then cool

your molten heels in waiting, another fill-up &
another, below a sky in tiger-orange shreds promoting change
of brakes & oil, twirling thumbs like universal joints & tying hands

in complex knots for which no merit badge was sewn. Yet sweat
it out a little longer—the final hour a frozen gearbox, a rusted lug nut refusing
    to turn—
the air hose hissing, like the Fiend Himself, incessantly

in your simple ear, urging you to cut out early, to take that first
transgressive bite of freedom, a pox on its hidden worm. But hang in there
an impossible moment more . . .

counting the drawer-closing minutes out,
like the pennies, nickels & dimes they were, for
Karen Franchi come stars, come cricket dark, full moon

of her shining arm's inoculation mark, for the two of us at last
to turn down some unpaved road & park
in her parents' Olds, with its padded elbow rests & seats

bouncing us on their cushioned knees, its power
locks & steering, arctic a/c, its glowing, 120-mile-per-hour promise
of 100-percent-pure American speed. She would shut the engine

but not the FM off, scroll the windows down, setting the polar spirits
free. They would scatter in a field of garter rocks & weed,
& before knowing it, we'd be intertwined like twins, alloys,

weft & warp, content & form, forming an ampersand of twisted clay
in every conceivable conjunction, fusing new contractions by closing the gap
between the sacred words of our once divided flesh. We would

cross & double-cross our ankles, arms, & lead us deeper
and deeper into temptation, without ever reaching its other, darker side—
fulfillment. We'd suck our bloods without breaking

the skin, leave pink carnations, roses, violets
on each other's throats, flowers on our childhoods' graves.
I'd be groping sightless, struggling to learn how to read

a bra clip's Braille, while Karen Franchi apprenticed
in the midwife's craft, nervous to deliver the undersized quintuplets
of my short-sleeve's buttons, her fingers quaking throughout those difficult

reverse births. Time would spin all three wheels
in a vital stasis, a here-&-now that gleamed like polished chrome.
A glorious present would come alive, inhaling the future, exhaling the past,

while keeping them invisible to us as summer breath. We would only know
the unescorted *this* of katydids, cantoring from balconies of trees,
of Wild Cherry's "Play that Funky Music," Rod Stewart's "Tonight's the Night,"

crossing whole oceans of air on rolling waves
to bow before the shrine we'd build
on the shining hill of every knuckle, at the confluence of our many-rivered
    palms,

bow, I said, before our temple of hair & bone, joint & nail,
fingerprints locking groove to groove. Which were you—her or me?
both or neither?—as little brothers & sisters dozed

in adolescence, while fathers & mothers slept in the same monarchical bed
yet still in separate rooms? Whom were you holding,
or withholding yourself from, while we would turn together, back & forth,
    side

to side, like a radio knob, trying to tune in through the static
to the single music we'd christen "our song"? Elders, literalists all,
called it "necking"; to us, it was "making out"—

a phrase that better captured the unlikely
success of the thing, our great dumb luck
in that scorching month we started kicking

our legs nearly out of their sockets, trying to kick them out of jeans
that clung like skins, placentas, as we clung to one another
like stitching & seam, space & ink, consequence & cause.

We were not haunted, you understand, by former lives, & had no adult sense
of ourselves as the houses (small closets even)
of ghosts. We were unaware of being rent in two

by tomorrow & yesterday—those siblings constantly warring
over the fragile doll that is one life. It was 1970-something,
we were seventeen, our days were not a series yet

of might-as-wells & might-have-beens. We were not anxious
over quandaries, wouldn't pick at them like splinters or scabs. & we
      didn't care,
didn't *think* to care, whether we would find our proper distance—

a berth wide enough, but not too wide, to keep us intimate, longing
for each other's next embrace. Because there was nothing
creeping up in our blind spots; no bottlenecks or wreckage lay in wait

ahead, & there could be nothing
false between us, nothing more than harmless alarms:
a stray dog scratching at the driver's side for scraps, dead branches

crashing down through living, our four ears perking up at first like rabbits'
then easing safely back into their warrens. Where, I wonder,
were you—in what mezzanine seated?—when we'd resume our dance

within the atomic dance, play within the cosmic play, me
the log-lugging grunt to her Prospero, patrician magician now
to her kindling hunter? What were you doing or thinking, while we'd pull off
      our

daring spectacles, fearlessly walking the high wire
between vexing contraries, swallowing the fires sparked by our two rough
      flints,
rubbings of our spindly limbs? Were you even paying attention enough

to warn us, before the double-barrel of that cruiser's head lamps swung over
our quick-ducked heads? Perhaps you could have cried out "Fuzz!"
or "Bacon!"—or simply whispered "Police"? But maybe

you had yet to feel the strain of staying
quiet, of keeping your lips buttoned after everything's been loosed.
Perhaps you didn't know, that far back, what it was like

for time, a stubborn zipper, to refuse to budge again,
no matter how hard you yanked with a wish
that furtive, gravel-crunching cruiser would pass on by

without paying you one pebble of mind. Though surely you know by now
that much of this never happened,
at least the way I say. You know whatever it is

we call love, or closeness, or just plain desire, appears
most luminescent, most clear, when the actual facts—those nagging skeeters,
swirling gnats—are swept away with a swish of the hand. &

you are perfectly aware
that before that great black-and-white can swim off into gray,
before I can tell how Karen Franchi & I

(or was it Carol Elliot, after all?) climbed out
onto the hood of her parents' pale green Olds,
or LTD, or Grand Marquis, after the law did

disappear, before I can describe the way we splayed ourselves
across that massive expanse of steel, with its rifle sight of an ornament
aimed at the enemy distance, or how we rested our naked backs

against a private beach of melted then super-cooled sand,
I'll have to come clean & admit there never was a cruiser,
& that I was certainly no cruiser myself. I will have to state for the record

that I was one who traveled strictly in a circle
of one, & spent my weekend nights with my family of four
speakers & Pioneer components, a harem of albums sprawled around me

on the floor—only my cravings & boredom moving back & forth, side
to side, like LEDs. I'll have to fess up
that all along the ampersands were me, seated cross-legged, in bashful

profile, unable to face beauty head on, to hear its harsh appraisal, its gavel
thwack, or listen to my heart shake loose & drop,
with a rattle & thunk, like a can in the station's Coke machine.

If that's "confessional," then you're a priest—
forgive. Forgive because you can, because we're all alone in this
together, every crime is ours, & not to forgive is the worst

we can commit. Perhaps that's over-righteous, so
forgive, & I'll repay, as best I can, with all five kingdoms
of the world: animal, vegetable, mineral, the kingdom of heaven

& the soundless void. I'll take you back to a golden age
before our words were dead, when "right on" & "radical"
leaped off our tongues with trapeze ease, when "fuck"s

were capable—imagine!—of "flying." I'll return us
to a time when you yourself had no idea
so much remains

split off from us, anonymous, that most things are known
by their aliases only, & that we might be nothing
more than our gropings toward & of each other in respective darks. Once,

you had no honest clue
that all the good intentions & acts of kindness in creation
don't stand a chance of halting the march of degradation & despair,

& vice versa. You couldn't fathom
what letting memory lead you to its waters meant: that it would make you
drink, would force your face down into & past your face, hold

your head beneath the surface until your lungs burst
into gasps of song. Think back: the nation had turned 200;
the fifty-first state shone white & full within what seemed like

our easy grasp. I told Karen Franchi if she looked closely
she could see the flag, waving in the solar wind. She said I lied,
& laughed. Knowing everything—that nothing—

I walked her through the zodiacal zoo, explained black holes,
their infinite, light-swallowing throats, told her there was no God,
no You, that human prayers were like those giant flares

flung out from then looping back to the sun. (I'd been reading Asimov
& Sartre.) She laughed again, & suddenly so did I, for no reason
I could name. Sometimes, I still hear that laughter of mine,

& it seems the only one I yet possess
not shot through with the cynical or cracked. Will you guffaw at my expense
if I confide that I have carried Karen Franchi's arm—

whether it was ever there or not—around my shoulder to this day,
& that some nights lying in bed, after snapping on
the dark, after distance (but not longing, never longing) closes down,
        I conjure her

& her parents' car, whatever make it was,
with its haloed tires, quadruple-barrel carburetor, windshield scarfed with tint,
with its glove box the size of the cradle, trunk as deep as the grave,

& I forget to worry if there is truly any greater good
than a single voice, anything more to life
than life itself. I simply believe in our communion, our laying on of hands

that would have made the purest of evangelists wince
with envy & delight. I believe
in the complete & unambiguous way I once believed in the accostive stink

of leaded fuel, in the tainting powers of grease,
the purifying of Go-Jo soap. & truthfully, I feel less afraid.
I am comforted, in fact, by how full we once were

of each other, how empty of ourselves,
& how we pressed our lips together, as if each kiss were our first
in, & our last for, many, many years.

STILL LIFE

> I will die in Paris, on a rainy day,
> on a day I already remember.
> —César Vallejo

My mind long gone, having forgot to shut
the body off, I will lie in some spare room,
some former nursery, entranced by waiting
for death to take me, but death will only take

its time. May will tap the pane, bring flowers
like no visitor, and by the hour the votive candle
of summer smolders out, and the leaves
catch flame, my dying will have taken on

a life of its own. I can hear my hollow cough,
smell my stench, decades away. Can you?
Can you tell me why we dare go on, knowing the end
is full, like the beginning, of gibberish and drool?

Early evenings in the living room,
steeped in shadow, the room of the living,
the daughter duty wills me to, some cardinal virtue
or old guilt consigns, will hear a shallow moan,

an infant tide, rise up through my throat.
(It must be the third or fourth year of my dying.)
She will patiently turn down, like a bed,
a page in her magazine, mount the stair,

and a boy to whom my name has fallen, like some
dashed twig, will help her tend my dying, clear
the feeding tube, spittle off my lip. He'll be told
to fetch warm water from the sink, and my wrinkled

white suit of skin will be cleansed, moot dignity
preserved. Perhaps one night the boy will search
my eyes, as his mother—divorced by then,
fed up with my dying—swabs away the sour milk

of age, or raise the shade and gaze outdoors
at trees, donning the dark like priests, and ponder
what awaits on the other side: blinding void,
or rapture, or both as in this life. Maybe he will pass

some time with tattered books, that lost year
of my dying, borrowed from my shelf.
Light in August will be his choice. Or
The Grapes of Wrath. He will journey back

to farms closed down like half my face,
one arm, after the stroke, crops that failed
unlike my heart, men and women giving up
their hopes, as my flesh will not (God knows

how much longer) its ghost. And if by chance
he stumbles on the diary I should bequeath
to fire, I pray the kid grows bored, sets the volume
back, before he comes across the section

on my own depression—maudlin, wrong—
starting in my late twenties, learns what I had
thought to do and almost done: end it all,
before anything whatsoever had begun.

END OF DAYS

There are those who swear it will start with the sun
snapping a fiery whip, lashing the hills with flame,
while others hear men and women shrieking,

being run through by burnished swords of wind,
scalding-hot needles of rain. They say lightning
will slash open the air with its serrated blade,

and thunder gallop like blood through the gash,
spewing steam from its blazing mane,
that a blinding radiance will pour down

the sky's domed walls, painting each town
a terrible, glaring red, stripping trees
and houses bare, and somewhere it is written

that windows will be left hanging
like limpid drapes. I'm not sure if parents
still recite how some will stand at the end of days,

rapt with terror, their stunned faces running off
their faces like tears, blistered arms and legs
wrapped in bandages of pure white heat,

seared eyes in blindfolds of light. Frankly,
I don't care. To me it's nothing more
than fancy run amok. I can't believe the children

will burn like wicks on the shores of molten rivers
(formerly the streets on which they played),
that the drunkard splayed in the gutter, leaning

against the curb-wall, will have his head struck
like a match. No, the stars and planets
will never gather, raise two candescent fists,

and pummel the darkness beyond recognition,
then stretch a tight clean sheet from this horizon
to that. Still, these visions toll like bells inside

my brain, and I can't help but eavesdrop
when someone dreams aloud
of witnessing the visage of God, or some other

lucid shadow, some maker of the void It fills,
hovering the punished plain. I'll never grasp the reason
elders sigh and worry their beards

over prophetic tomes, why the wisest of women
can be found at tables lit by a single candle,
thinking its tiny torch our collective future

writ small. Yet to hear the haunting yowl
of the unspayed cat in spring, walking
her fertility's coals, or to pass a cluster of teens

puffing on cigarettes, and watch the halos
of their smoke rings warp, then vanish
into nowhere, is to gain a flickering sense

of what it suddenly might mean
to have been handed down a tale that binds
people together, twisting the many

strands of their mortal fears
into a rope that might be lowered when they fall
into the dark abysses of their making.

It's to have some notion why
the handful of survivors, scattered across
the deserted land, are predicted to go crazy,

finding it impossible to face the stark
field sprawled before their sight, and shooting
themselves toward heaven like flares.

HOW IT HAPPENED

We watched the metal fire spread
through distant streets, cities covered by smoke
and CNN, buildings reduced to rubble and our 24-inch screens.
We studied the morning papers, theories of reporters,
took their correspondence course
in war. Photos showed us faces
annexed by the dust. We'd gasp for the air
they couldn't. Our minds became occupied
territories, and the wrinkles in our brows deepened like wounds.
We would stand eye to eye at the mirror,
stare down our fear in the glass.
One night, a woman wept into her pillow
over the spilled milk of another woman's body.
Her heart felt empty, though it lost no blood.
Someone lit a candle as an act of resistance
against the dark. Another slit a finger chopping onions
and the prophecy came true.
Who could sense a gentle breeze
stirring hair, blouses, the branches of a dogwood overhead?
We would find no excuses, solace in distance.
How could we allow the light of spring
to strike our cheeks so mildly
and not rebel? We had no sex to honor those degraded,
traded passion for compassion
and suffered, with pride, our losses. Then
one man set down his fork and spoke:

"Perhaps our peace is false. Still,
it's peace." And the voice swept through our residences, spread
like a fire of steel. Ardently, someone swore
to endure, then punished her mouth for swearing.
Our innards learned to untie the knots
they'd gotten themselves into. No longer
were our tongues the red carpets
on which convictions walked like kings. We passed like ghosts
through gray walls of steam, into soothing showers.
Lulled by radio on the route to work,
choice became the war
our minds refused to make.
We breathed in Sunday afternoon
for the anesthesia it bestows. Time lengthened with our shadows
as the house of summer burned slowly to the ground.
Those shadows looked like airstrips,
food lines, trains to remove the innocents . . .
paths out of ourselves for the taking.

HOW TO BEGIN
A POETRY READING

Begin with a poem by a friend of yours, one
who still remembers the moonless nights you bartered
fruit and cigarettes for a chain of whispers,

who refuses to elide the way you huddled,
years ago, in the corners of bent arms, sunken chests,
and how it seemed as though your spines,

whenever the distance lifted an anguished cry,
were yanked on like ropes—causing the bells
of hardened hearts to sound their muffled alarms.

Start off with a poem by a friend who recollects
the promises of bellows-throated elders, moot
guarantees the neighbors clutched like infants,

rumors that made their ears catch fire,
then gradually (as one day dropped its coal
into the next) flutter off . . . ash-colored moths.

One assumes the unspeakable impossible to forget.
The unspeakable is not impossible to forget.
That's why it's best to begin with a poem by a friend

who wouldn't flinch in shimmering darkness
when hired bruisers, volunteer thugs, threatened
to clip the tongue's one wing, who remained convinced

it would grow back stronger, capable of longer flights.
How could anyone not listen closely? What audience
would have the nerve to crinkle bags, whisper

behind curved palms? Especially when we're talking
about a friend who still recalls the shadows
of stray dogs clinging to walls

like waifs to the legs of well-heeled passersby,
how the sun would swing overhead at noon
like a light-filled noose, near nightfall like a gutted hare on a hook

in a Flemish master's portrait of opulence.
At times, the invisible itself appeared
charged with frenetic motion. Alder trees

threw tantrums, collapsed into leafy seizures,
while no wind blew. Later, nothing moved,
as though time were nothing more than the watch

that kept it—the watch someone had neglected
or declined to wind. It's tempting to set all that
aside, to lower slowly, soothingly, into

oblivion's warm bath. It's natural to want to
shove into cupboards—like cherished books,
ancestors' loose jewels—the nagging questions of old:

Should we have entered further into
or come out of hiding? Were we foolishly
hemmed in by the very squares we strove to think

outside of? Certainly you've earned the right
to select amnesia over vigilance, relentless dwelling.
Hence the need for a poem by a friend

devoted to the damaged, lost, and pilfered goods.
Who can bear to hear of hawthorns
gleaming with blackness on autumn nights,

or put up with paeans to hydrangeas,
yellow pansies, phlox—unless they're firmly
rooted in the darkest of soils? I thrill

to the goshawk boarding air, to fluted labors
of the thrush in dusk's obscurities. I believe every
true utterance, however small, a possible title

for the whole of the world. But I am haunted
by a past of filling too many hours' holes
with terrified premonitions, prophecies of gloom,

and can't seem to find a way to look beyond
the pupil eclipsing what luminescence burns
behind each eye. That's why I choose to start

with a poem by a friend—one wet
behind the ears, down the cheek—a friend
I've longed (for too long now) to possess, be.

THE SIGN

A few days after their mother's mind, like a rotten beam, started giving
way, they hastened home to stand, hushed as bedposts, beside her,
to hold her hand exactly unlike lovers, and wait, among the dust
and rubble of her caving in, all of them who thought they knew
what family meant—caulk and buttresses, blood thicker than stone—
for a sign to haul her off to the other home, deposit her with the other

wreckage, not one of them knowing which would consent
to give that sign, that gift, each convinced it would take another,
or how the sign would manifest itself: a daughter's fist
sledging a tabletop at supper, an outbreak of tears, maybe
simply the words "It's time," in a voice exhausted from the climb
out of the pit of its speaker's throat. It had snowed the night before,

and the eldest, her only son, trudged out front to clear
the walk, with any luck his head. Balding, overfed,
he bent into the job with everything he could muster up
of the prime he knew he'd never really had. He leaned into it
with something like determination, but more opaque, not yet that
sure of itself. Slowly, he brought the path to his mother's stoop back

in view, removing the coldness from his body and the cracked
cement, both of them steaming in the sun. Slowly, he worked
himself into isolation, deaf to the rasp of metal across concrete,
blind to fatigue, until finally he'd hefted the last shovelful
on the mound. It was then he spotted the window, high on the house,
someone had smashed in. His blood flared when he thought

of all the bill-burgeoning heat being sucked away
by the vast blue lung of the sky, how he'd have to haul himself
up to the attic, hunch in dust, yank the jagged teeth of glass
from their wooden frame, break some more of his aching back.
He cursed the local punk, spoiled with youth, who must have
hurled a snowball from the street, the misfires it must have taken

till the kid got it right. He could hear the hollow thwacks
against siding, scaring the old woman he loved inside half
to death, when half to death for her meant half an inch.
He grasped the shovel by the throat and started choking.
But suddenly the anger left him, and everything was silent,
sheer trajectory and perfect arc. He saw what appeared to be

pure flight, as if somehow he'd become that icy sphere
leaving a gloved hand, finding a groove in air between the forces
of gravity and a young boy's arm. And he felt what had to be
pure breakage, one clarity shattered, painlessly,
by another. Far in the back of his mind, he knew nothing
like this had ever happened to him, never would again,

that he was going through something so new and different
he had both to instruct and apprentice for himself.
Then it stopped, and he snapped alert,
a scarf of breath streaming from his mouth.
A winter bird sliced past, the negative scent of cold.
It had come, he thought: the sign he had prayed for

so far under his breath it couldn't rise to shame him.
He wheeled to make his way indoors, bear witness
to the others. His sister met him in the drive,
chin lowered, jacketless, her eyes both meeting
and averting his. She didn't speak, only shook her head.
The sign, he realized, had been misread.

50

W O R K

This afternoon, my father is working
in the rock garden I helped him plant
back when we were kids. He's stabbing
his trowel into Pennsylvania, the small plot
I own now, displacing the dirt as his body did
before my heart was ready. I sit watching
from the screened-in porch, serving
as his ghost's witness, doing that work.
My father and I are sharing our love
of privacy together, as we often would
when separation was still a window screen
that could be lifted. An April breeze hangs
in the neighbor's dogwood. The scent
of the dogwood hangs in the breeze.
So my father hikes up his pant legs,
plants one knee in dankness, yanks
a menacing weed. "It's choking my arabis,"
his hands are saying, "so it must be strangled,"
his hands of justice that, thank God,
never fell on me. Kneeling like this,
my father is worshipping again
in the only church he ever trusted.
That's right, pop, tear away at the earth
you loved. "Each prayer," I tell myself,
"is an act of removal," and wait
to learn what it means. A cardinal,

male, sweeps down from the sky
to show off his crimson miter.
He's brought along his sermon, his *tik-tik
tik-tik*. Praise to that. Praise to grass
for getting stomped on, day after day,
and never once complaining. Praise to names
like "arabis" and "Sisyphus," whom my father
is impersonating now, hefting an infant
boulder in the sun. Work: it's all that does,
all that keeps us focused on the real.
It's what we're here for, nothing more
or less. Here comes some now.
Carl, the postman, carries himself
up the driveway with the world
on his shoulder, I hope. I want words
of passion and passionate denial from Milan
and Buenos Aires, though I'm loveless
in both cities. He passes by my father
but doesn't wave, because Carl knows his job,
his route, who's alive on it, who's not.
He greets me and hands over the electric bill,
a come-on from American Express,
the monthly allowance from my father,
signed by Prudential Life. And now I'm wondering
about the work it takes to set things
aside, to save, instead of blowing everything
you've earned on everything you can,
to plan for the future of your work,
insure it will not vanish, as the postman has,
and the cardinal. "Everything worthwhile,"
I think, "takes time, and time takes
everything worthwhile," but banish the thought
because I know what it means. Dad,
take off those soiled leather gloves. Come
shake my hand, fill it with your sweat.
Embrace me as a father should an eldest son.
Lean that spade against the ground. I'll take it up
for you some day. Your work is done.

LOSING FATHER'S POCKETWATCH

I lean to heft the anchor in, when *oh,*
it's gone . . . spinning down gold,
to copper, to black, into the crappie hole,
and cold terror climbs the rungs of my spine.

After father learns, he stands like a sentry
on the dock. Night drifts up slow, a glacier
of coal, as he surveys the jade-black lake,
breath pouring thick from the chimney
of his throat. It seems time has stopped,
or turns underwater in the watch alone.

Rooted on porch steps, I witness him
strip his shirt, bend, and dip flannel
to cool his severe brow. By now, the sky
is a massive anvil, and I wish I'd hammered

the watch to dust, mangled the hands
before his eyes till he slapped me hard.
Instead, he spears out arms and buries
himself in water, hopelessly kicking
toward the hole, the sharp smacks
of his strokes ringing the air.

BLUEGILLS

The end of the summer Uncle Puding died
you hung a day's worth from the aspen nail
watched them gulp the dimming air,
flap off bark, rattle the stringer chain.
You let dorsals slowly unfan, tails stiffen
and curl, and midges dart the gills, which gaped
and shut like mouths in some silent quarrel
with what was coming on, scentless,
quiet as time. You wanted to feel afraid
(black water lapping the algaed bank)
and gazed into the gilltips, glowing past dusk,
blue as dragonflies, blue as butane flame,
yet sensed no heat when you steadied
a finger near. And when you stretched
to stroke the gills wrong, backwards
for a nick, no blood came, no sweat
in cool sleeves down your face
or sudden screak of pain—only wind
dwelling in the reeds, and a heron,
far off, slicing open water for a meal.
Why didn't you think then to slip
the whole catch back, into the lilies,
under the dock? Why did you pause
until jaws and eyes locked wide for good,
looking as though the end were a surprise?

BLOOD WORK

> Clay lies still, but blood's a rover . . .
>
> —A. E. Housman

Jane Noone, R.N.,
velcroes the pressure tester
and pumps (your fist tenses)
and pumps and pumps

till you hear mother breathing,
wheezing in the red
frenzy of birth, squeezing you
out, October 5th, late.

Jane finds the blue root
of your arm-crook. You feel the thud,
thud, thud of pulse, and it's your father
blundering drunk down porch steps,

his head lit like a torch. You rush
to help, but Jane needles well,
and the dark milk of your body
swirls the tube. Father's eyes

whirl: he slips and he
falls and slits open his brow
easy as a letter. You crouch nearby
(his face is a butcher's apron)

as Jane Noone withdraws the silver tip
and alcohol and cotton halt the drip.

G L A S S

The summer we first drank the clear blood
of juniper berries, and took our first hard pulls
of bourbon and rye, sucking the hot milk down
in long, amber waves of distilled grain.
Our balls were made of brass—one copper,
one zinc—and we drove around in circles
hooting like dogs at shadows,
then over three towns to the quarry
to holler for those we howled to undress,
just to hear walled rock repeat their names.
We'd guzzle Mad Dog 20/20, till our words
and vision blurred, from bottles looking
nothing like the ones that glistened
in the constant morning sun of the 1950s,
on the porches of our parents' childhood homes.
The summer we first learned you are
what you drink from. Their bottles had rounded
shoulders, soft, full mouths—were honest, homogenized,
knew zero of itching desire. They were devoted
to sturdy bodies, fortified souls.
Ours were rectangular, biting at the lip,
screw-topped. We drew them from secret pouches
in our jean jackets. Pints of Comfort
hugged our asses in place of wallets.
We dared anyone to pick our pockets.
The summer we discovered you are what can be

jerked out brashly and shared, what must be held
with fingers and thumbs at hard right angles,
never in any nurturing, cradle-like grip. The summer
we were still unbroken, smooth as glass.

R E J O I C E

for S. M.

It's time to clear the cobwebs from our throats, and voice
the simple truth (which thankfully never is) that the world's not just
in orbit around the sun, but also set by an unnamed source
to swing—*Amen*—between two poles. One bright hour, like an odds-on horse,
gallops and breaks the tape; the next falls lame and must
be shot, dragged into time's common grave.
Ocean artfully sculpts the rock, which shatters the cresting wave,
unconcerned with who we are or would become. Rejoice.

Rejoice that every sacrifice demands
an elevation, that each cruel twist (of knife, fate, wrist) vouches for
one good turn. Sure, it's hard not to fret: Are we fiery or merely settling dust,
animate with something more than naked will,
or the subjects, strictly, in a traveling exhibition of fig-leafed nudes, still
lifes? Many fear that they are living in inertia's sin, that their longings rust
inside them—buried, like hatchets, after years of making war
with their consciences. But let us bow our heads in praise, join hands,

not despite but because of such vexations. Let's pay
due homage to our griefs for what they are: gifts that keep on giving
off their opposites, in perfect inverse degrees.
How could we appreciate, without them, the fluent expertise
of sap-gum and slippery elm, serving as interpreters of the four living
winds, or suitably admire the fealty of the shadow,

how loyally it guards the master flesh? The mundane presses forward, all day,
making us recoil at dangerous backward angles. Tomorrow,

some are certain to feel poisoned, or like poison
to something trying violently to reject them. None
of this can be denied. And yet confess: who really places
faith in a realm apart from ruin? Who thinks we'd bother claiming what we
cherish or desire (barely convinced ourselves), or keep searching each
        other's surfaces
for doors that might be opened with a tongue or finger's key,
if every one of us in this ink-bespattered room hadn't tried, and
        dolefully failed,
to turn the daily dross to gold—if none had ever jailed

and left himself for dead, weeping in winter, peering out from
behind lucid bars? Take these lovers by the foaming sea,
watching it beat itself against the strand
like clothes refusing to come
clean. Say at noon they stare directly at the sun, until it starts to ring
with pain inside their ears. Or say they hear it shriek at dusk, going
down in its own flames. Isn't this the sound (racking, almost beastly)
that leads them, on heading home, to marvel at the tranquil sand,

how the beach retains so well
where they have moved? Let's strip, with that in mind,
the glossy veneers from off our
faces, pull reticence up by
its roots like a rotten tooth. May we speak the words that cower
at the back of the mouth, behind
the uvula's ever-suspended tear, and glorify
our fruitless efforts and fallings short. We should thrill to tell

the tale of how we struggled to survive the drought
and record heat last summer, without
losing our marbles or cools—how the forty days and nights
of August finally wore us down, and we ended up in petty fights,
driving accusations into one another
like nails. Who will give the benediction of other

botched attempts? I myself have flubbed and missed
the mark on many things I am grateful for. Repeatedly, I've pissed

in the trough from which I drink,
and can't begin to think
how often I've lost track of the motions of the inner spheres,
of a heart that spins on a crooked rod, of my soul's small
ball
of ice and fire. Perhaps you've faced like troubles of your own? Don't frown,
or figure these for rantings of a morbid clown.
If it weren't for gaffes, ineptitudes like these, what cheers

could we devise for clinking glasses, what blisses
would we know? We'd scarcely feel the warming blaze of
hearths in bitter cold, or kisses
so incendiary they turn the lip to flame. We'd have no way to rate
the fragrance of gardenia, lilac, lily of the valley,
never having stopped to smell the festering rose. And surely there'd be
no means to savor favorite fruits, plums and tangerines, vegetables we love.
I'm thinking of asparagus, of buttered spears with paint-brush tips
    that illuminate

our mouths' domed ceilings, and acorn squashes served piping hot
in their dark green bowls. Or I'm thinking that it's nearly dawn, and you are
dreaming of the dead moon in your arms, of carrying it to the top of some far
hill to plant its bulb, believing it will blossom in a dozen hours,
spill petals on your head in incandescent showers.
Tell me, though: what aerial blessings could ever
descend in soothing mists, if not
for outbursts of foul-tempered clouds, if thunderstorms never

kicked over potted plants on stoops, snapped flowers' tender
necks, or punched umbrellas inside out until their slender
bones and tendons showed? Who could even prove if any dreamspun
wish were granted, without the torments of
the very old, hardly tempered by repetition,
the apprentice agonies of children? Once, there was a boy, ball glove
in hand. He sat alone at his bedroom window on a dreary April day—not crying,
but looking as though he were dying

of rain. Kneel tonight beside the altar of your single or half-empty double bed, and say
aloud, if you remember how,
your prayers. (Ignore for now
the doubt that flaps and scratches like a maddened bat
in the belfry of your steepled hands.) Pray to woes
not only of the boy, but of those
in their late teens and early twenties. Soon they will begin to hack away
at the past, turning their parents into monsters, before turning into their parents. Here's to that.

Here's to tortures we've endured while living apart, you and I.
Even though we're able to conceal each scar
with a smile, for as long sometimes as an afternoon, nonetheless
the stitch marks show
on our cracked lips, belying facile joy. For once, let's not evade: we are
lonely, every one of us, and frightened, those who deny
it, most of all. We sew
on patches to cover stains, and yes,

one of us is destined (this week, maybe next) to climb
to the highest western margin
of a teeming city or country town, to watch with sadness and a wistful eye
the capsized, deep blue ship of the sky
sink over the horizon's edge—and to grow afraid. If I'm
that chosen son, then I can only hope to feel
my body hauled beneath the rising half-moon's keel,
my entire being held in

a single breath, clung to like a slippery rope. Imagine the ecstasies bound
to issue from such a trial—what with doom and gloom
being rapture's bride and boutonniered groom.
Consider the flowers of evil, one of which is clipped today
from a gentle woman's breast, another found
in a couple months behind the one removed. Rejoice that she won't find
a way
to stop from wondering if
her single life, when it drops itself at last—a handkerchief

embroidered with the ornate pattern of her veins—will be
taken up by courtier God or indifferent void, if featureless space will fill
her chest, like an inexhalable breath, or
the divine inspire. Praise that every minute, several more fall ill,
knowing themselves their own disease and only cure,
that spring cannot break ground with its first shoot
without recalling a brother's spine (his brain's one root)
stunted, or the seed of his unborn body

sprouting atrophied limbs. It's time to honor the promises—friend, foe—
you never kept, alleging they escaped your mind, while all along they
    were free
to wander off into the thin air of which they were made.
Time to say the grace of your well-misspent youth. How tendentious
    and devout
you were, so full of pious verities and other virtues that graciously
proved uneasy, how profoundly in the dark about
what would, eventually, come easiest of all: for you to let yourself go
blind to the prospects of this earthly muck and murk, for a haughty silence to
    masquerade

as The Unsayable. Let's celebrate your
having lost a narrow, gained a Gordian, way. We're happily all the more
confounded for it. And now that I sincerely feel at the heights and depths of
    my powers,
let's rejoice, here at the close, in the halting, exalting, blear- and
    clear-eyed hours
it took to put this simple
thing together. Then let's praise again, as from the start, that everything
is anything
but simple.

three

STRANGE PIETÀ

> If any state be enviable on earth,
> 'Tis yon born idiot's, who, as days go by,
> Still rubs his hands before him, like a fly,
> In a queer sort of meditative mirth.
> > —George Meredith

> As for the exposure and rearing of children,
> let there be a law that no deformed child shall live.
> > —Aristotle, The Politics

1.

When, in the shallows of late afternoon,
light's low tide, where he floats each day, face-
down in his locked chair, having flailed for hours
and failed again to reach the shore of the other

world—the world (if you can cast eyes in inky
schools like these, reel in your limit when you please
to sense) chance lets us share—or from the depths
of a late-night sleep, bundled in a state-owned bed,

his headboard not yet stone, my brother breaches
for one brief gasp, one empty lunge for the splintered
plank his turn has been, and starts, in a swoop
of eyelids, to sink into memory, that dingy pond;

when, in his final act, he enters the fifth season,
drains himself of urine and shit, saliva and snot,

gives up those ghosts, and is pronounced innocent,
as he has been from the very instant of being

placed in the double jeopardy of ovum and sperm,
through the ill-set terms of his life sentence,
with its misplaced modifiers, bungled punctuations,
to his release from the padded cell of our mother's flesh;

when he is delivered, irreversibly, from the bondage
of tendon and bone, surgically tightened dressings of skin,
of feet that never once will knock the black-and-white
globe through tended posts, kick to an island of boards

on the upstate lake whose flawless mimesis of sky
I angled summers with bow and oar and bobbered line;
when he sheds the limits of legs that are their fetters,
arms that cannot, no matter how hard they tug,

yank themselves free from irregular sleeves, hands
that won't mend engines, glide ivory or lettered keys,
silk of a lover's cheek, because there are no miracles
in this life except this life, because debility's logic

and ethics are strict: *Two wrongs can't make a right;*
then, our family will congregate, as we have today,
to commemorate independence, and drown our griefs
for the runts they've been, only to watch them rise,

phoenixes dripping not fire but the wedding of ice and fire,
rise, against the backdrop of a past that must come
again, not second any more, against the gravity, as well,
of my brother's inhuman condition, and because of it.

2.

Because of it, I float on a pool of shade, a collapsible
chair of my own—head bent too, not in fatigue
but "loveroot, silkthread," the "feeling of health"
in democracy's Song of Songs (my annual running

through on "fourth of Seventh-month"). On the other
side of the yard, aunts and uncles, younger cousins,
a grandmother still a few years shy of her first
Parkinson's twitch, scan skies instead, anxiously

awaiting the twist in the plot of weather prefigured
in the morning paper. They know well the false
rhetoric of climate, the unearthly's unstable text—
beach vacations botched gray, campsites down the slope

of a hill squalled under—and can't help denying
the total absence of cloud hanging over their heads,
this birch's atrophied leaves and limbs, damp air paralyzed
from its pale neck down. It seems I alone can trust

that only faces and bottles of beer will blur with wetness
today, that no one's crown will wear thorns of rain.
Worry, for my family, is a form of prayer. Working
strands like the rosary that lapsed from her hands

decades back, my mother weaves her granddaughter
into braids. She's entreating the day stay clear
as maxim, so Jessie can attend real fireworks tonight,
not the kid's stuff of sparklers throwing tantrums

of light in her grasp, that small thrill made smaller
by grown-up caution. Prickly as impatience,
another degree inches my arm—inky-dinky spider—
causing my attention to miss a turn, drift

into mirage: the stumpy bus's brakes sighing
to a halt at the curb, a second set of wheels starting
to roll. And isn't that just it: isn't it our anticipations
that principally divide us—for them, weather without

pattern that won't arrive, for me, a brother without
same who will? If freedom's holy, this is the first
minor holiday he'll celebrate with us since moving
back East from Pittsburgh, in the season of blood,

not migration. Four Easters now, three Thanksgivings
and Christmases of mis-strung popcorn, scotch tape
and ribbons that foil, he's spent among our struggles
to act normal around him. Believe me, it's not easy

when normal's what shames you, when each act
coming off without the slightest hitch or doubt about success
breeds consequence obscene as flies
that must be shooed off cookout food. It takes

practice, unflagging will—practice that never will
make perfect, will that won't shoulder one of us
above reproach, and "to again come close to" is,
in this case, to warrant blame. Overhead, cicadas

give voice to heat; the local grackle heckles
the grounded. Should I tell them *Quiet,* that no one song
or dissonance is large enough for enough to hear?
Should I ask them why, when we mean luck

we say, "redemption through suffering and love"?
My gaze returns to the page, falls on the phrase
"with halfshut eyes bent sideways," and that, as if
designed, is how I suddenly glimpse my brother

Tom's six-year-old, skipping across the top of the lawn
like a stone. *Uncle Greg!* she's calling, pointing
towards the garage, *Come look!* She yanks my hand
(I drop Walt in the "summer grass" he leaned on

like a shoulder) and weaves me like no brief lyric
over minefields of scattered toys and anthills,
through a weathered side door still holding on
by a single hinge, mote galaxies, the barbed stink

of gasoline, then pokes a finger up to dimness
where two beams cradle the bowl of twigs her smile
half-begs, half-orders me to climb to and scout
for eggs. At this age, most skirt such ill-lit places,

pegboards fanged with ripsaws and Phillips heads,
chisels and awls, the green irises of a carpenter's level
stalking from a hanging shelf, but my niece is fearless
with curiosity, and won't hear it when I launch into

adult facts: it's the 4th of July, the young hatched
in April or May, are long gone by now. Jessie wants
action, not explanation, and who can blame her?
Before I know it, I've taken three rickety rungs

into the role I've been chosen for, peer precariously
over the edge. *Empty,* I report . . . but stepping down
I spot, behind a leaning tower of *National Geographics*,
what she has not: a lost chapter of natural history,

still being edited by a red-eyed team of flies.
Empty, I say again, slowly guiding her outside,
one palm on her upper back, in the space below
the neck, between her own stunted wings.

3.

A few weeks after Jessie's other uncle was born,
forms were signed that jettisoned him into the arms
of Mercy's siblings, Jesus' wives. While I am "Uncle Greg"
to her, my brother is simply "Jonathan," as though

mental trumps physical age in heredity's game of Pitch.
I had just turned six myself, two voids at the front
of my mouth, one about to sprout at the back, when
my mother stepped to the curb with only her face

in her hands, clapped there as if to keep it from sliding
off. I may remember skin as pale as the plastic bracelet,
charmed with the letters of her licensed name, still clasped
around one wrist, and how, after the storm door rattled

shut, there fell one of those silences you never stop
hearing, that never stops falling. Clutching the banister
of my father's arm, she slouched upstairs, crawled
inside the folds of their queen-sized bed, and began

to read the ceiling like a post-war novel, becoming
the hero of its blank pages. For days that mocked
weeks (time, a clogged IV), at the hour walls
and too-staged family portraits fuse, when mirrors tint

inward and windows focused east begin, like budding
prophets, to lose their sight—blurring dogwoods still
a month away from opening their tight, five-petalled fists
to sign the yearly armistice with frost—my mother in a prison

suit of shadow and sunlight through half-tipped blinds
would reach another chapter's end, and the final period
of that day's installment, like either of her pupils
in the fraying light, would dilate, and keep on dilating,

until she could not be read. Or were those black holes
drawing the fading radiance inside their massive absences?
Was that the reason she kept the color of cloud?
I'm only sure of flying five sidewalks home each afternoon

from Sister Bernadette, whose wooden pointer I'd followed
with the utmost care of the petrified, as it made its daily
pilgrimage from the board on which it rapped the Ten
C's and Seven Deadly S's, the alphabet of fear,

to the backs of Tony Cannetta's hands, to study
my mother through a door three-quarters shut, guarded
by paternal rule forbidding access, to do my first real
homework: scanning the two- and three-line sapphics

the pillow had scrawled on the side of her face
since breakfast bowls clacked in the sink. I'll translate
none, but wonder how many scrawny verses I've pillowed
since then in her name, as I wonder how my father,

in that first term of grief, survived his own difficult
labor—the painful, drawn-out delivery of explanation.
My mind's eye blinks, and if I squint into the stringent
light of three decades gone to flame, I can see him

racing to the telephone whenever it cried out
in its sleep, gently lifting the handset, speaking
softly in its twelve-lobed ear, swaddling the ugly
facts in apothegms and whispers, then placing it

down for another nap. I can make out stretch
marks lengthening on his temples and brow
as he tends the questions and concerns of distant
relatives, close friends, hear again the nerves unraveling

at the end of his voice's rope, the terms "spina bifida,"
"shunt," forming warped halos of sound without sense
above my eavesdropping ears. If I must, I can recall
the way his mouth would hang (and I must) like a windless

flag after hanging up, how he'd cover his own face
with a prayer book of palms, mumble hermeneutics
of their dark lines. Dusks, after work with bindings
and must, foxed card catalogs, bespectacled spinsters,

he'd idle alone on the square of cement that served
as back yard then, watching the last of our mother
star run over the horizon's edge. Later, after something
Swanson with his two other musketeers, or some

Samaritan casserole tasting of consolation, he'd fix
a plate of buttered toast, two mugs of steam
(his under-eyes the very hue of used tea bags)
and wobble a tray upstairs, force my mother to eat,

or concede she should. My brother who can and I
would stand on the threshold of bulb light at their door's

foot, green Galileos peering through the keyhole:
strange pietà. Over the next ten years, the marriage

would become a kind of Zeno's paradox of hearts
that never could quite come together, and throughout
my teens they'd often squabble, over money mostly—
perhaps because it cost them less than bickerings

about in-laws, us kids, or why their bed stopped
banging its head against the wall our two rooms shared.
But those nights we'd overhear assurances
that things would work out for the best, proof

that reductions are the grandest of exaggerations. Usually,
my mother would heave sighs of doubt, her breath the sound
of grace falling from itself, but some nights she'd grow
too full of hope's warm formula, vomit it back

in my father's lap, cursing the world and its false
covenants, taking my other Father's name and pitching
it like dishware, cheap crockery, around the place.
We heard her swear at the top and over the top of her lungs

that she'd never conceive again, making herself
barren with a vow, a pledge of allegiance to sterility.
This, I guess in reverse, was how she became a Bertha
in the attic of at least one boyhood head,

how I came to fear she'd never come fully home.
But I was in first grade then—March 1970—
and couldn't calculate the tangents and trajectories
of resilience yet, let alone the length of time it takes

for such a tiny ball of light as the human soul to reach
the bottom of inner space, and reflect out of the pit
it makes descending. Under a quilt of many colors,
I tossed awake one night in my lower bunk, the cold dark

dropping and dropping behind the panes—past
midnight, past freezing. I lay dreaming with open eyes
of the thermometer outside the kitchen door
having its blood drawn without pain, crossing my fingers

and myself for one last snow to cancel streets
and school, not just fire hydrants and the hoods of cars.
I listened to the sharpened nails of wind
pluck power wires, and the hiss of coiled iron

in the corner's double-darkness, the *drip, drip, drip*
of the bathroom faucet torturing the drain, keeping
the house's arteries from bursting, the low thunder
of my father's sleep. Then, bare floorboards winced.

Slippered steps entered the other adjacent room
(unnecessary nursery), and came to a halt abruptly,
their echoes slackening into stillness, like flags losing
hold of a breeze. I started to climb from bed, but

a bellow tore the quiet I intended to keep, seeming
to slit the throat that sent it, leaving a gash that would
take a life to heal, a sound whose waves ripple still,
its initial ring with a radius over twenty years wide.

Whether my mother burst into sobs or laughter, I can't say,
or won't. Cold feet had carried me to the brink of my room,
courage. *Mom?* I throw my voice over that verge again.
I'm fine, the mind's ear returns. *Go back to bed.*

4.

He wears a chest of spangles and an Aide-for-a-Day
grips the drooping union on a stick. I turn back
to the present, witness him wheel the drive,
making each inch of ascent by hand, sweet craftsman.

Along with Jessie's cry in the middle distance—
Jonathan is here!—I hear my calling to him

75

from inward, one voice shouldering through a rabble
of selves, and sooner than I'd think, I'm running

fingers through muss, clenching the padded handles
that jut from his back like wings. I'm filling my role
as elder sibling, unpaid aide, rolling him
around to our gathering of photogenic looks

under the sky's wide aperture, his slouched double
riding shotgun on the lawn. I'm walking the parallel
tracks that are my brother's footprints in grass, grooves
I shunt to the left to avoid an orphaned Barbie.

No, I'm Greg. You remember me. I've rocked you
in the overturned cradle of my skull since the day,
like a coin for luck, you were dropped into our fickle pool.
If only you could grasp how much you've grown

inside me, like an extra lung, taught me how
to breathe in carbon black, date half lives. Here's a tip,
for remuneration, from your big brother: doubt
those who rush to hug and fawn. Bounding to you

is away from where the honest would rather go.
I can raise either of my right hands and testify
to greetings more awkward than your crayoned
autograph, to flawed attempts at putting ourselves

in your pointless shoes, lips that lie not with the shapes
of sound, but with those they put on. I've read countless
lines of eye contact wear thin and snap, seen each of us
teeter across other invisible tightropes, searching

for the fragile balance between the heart that goes out
to your mangled man-child body, and the one
that lurches from it. Your laugh, dearly beloved,
like the disease that freed it, is not contagious.

Its life-rattle works on others' glee like vaccine.
I'm determined, nonetheless, to start the fun,
have conjured up an Ariel in myself to trick
fear out of my proportion, close the distance

that opens as it shrinks. Don't be afraid if I dare
to play to your very real extended adolescence,
tipping you back in a wheelie to race hedges,
the side yard's potted spider plants and ferns. Already,

we've lost: play's latest prodigy is performing *calisthenics*
on gym mats of grass, unmindful you will never realize
either of that word's Greek roots. She's putting on
a show of acrobatics, unexamined pride, raising arms,

as though at gun point, throwing them down and kicking
herself in the space just lit with a smile, tumbling
with no compunction—a four-spoked shaky wheel.
Both her sets of parents, the young and not so young,

applaud from wicker, naming her flaws precious,
shouting, *Beautiful, Jes!* and this time I find myself
agreeing: beauty must be that which can't be borrowed
or sought, which must be fallen into during carefree

exercise. And now she's making you cackle, Jon,
and that's all that matters—anyone tell me no—
in this world crutched on either side by the inanimate.
We all know you'll give a hundred lousy performances

today, spew corn on the cob like confetti in parades
downtown, soil Depends, that the rail-thin arm
and frail-fingered hand of at least one plastic fork
will escape your own. The Heinz regime is certain

to annex a dozen states from the front of your shirt.
We know that if a group shot gets snapped, your neck
may well reveal its photographic memory of where
the shunt has been installed. Don't forget to pardon

yourself after slurping, burping Sprite. And any one of us
can prophesy that before the elders stop speaking
in nostalgia's tongue—with its single tense, the past
perfect—before they quit reminiscing about each other,

others who've "passed away," still others whose faces
and names hide behind time, your lids will flutter
at half mast, head sway that way and this, as if tracking
Meredith's fly, which you couldn't swat in a lifetime

without a hand from happenstance. The slender
filament connecting you to us will sizzle in two,
your gaze drop off in your lap. We know that
by the time the day's fever breaks, birch clasps with

dusk, and the west swallows whole its morsel of fire
without choking or drool, your two brothers will slobber,
as well—not cole slaw or baked beans, hamburger patties
with their backs lashed black by the grill, Bomb-Pops

or cherry jello made patriotic with blueberries and baby
marshmallows, but words, after downing a fifth of sour mash
together, a couple six-packs of Rolling Rock. We know that
before mosquitoes hatch from absence, and the yard sends

up its insect flares, signaling us to stuff the Coleman
full of ice and soda, the station wagon with folded
blankets and chaise longues, drive out to Narberth Park,
before we spread ourselves like a feast beneath an inverted

blue Depression glass bowl of sky (the first stars'
bright tautologies affirming the deathless consequent
of light), and wait for lambent shrapnel to spray down
on our heads like blessings, one of those brothers

will recede from the family picture—too Rockwell
for his tastes—become mute, opaque, his own hiding

place, while the other inspects the empty bottle's throat,
holding it to one eye, a kaleidoscope of voids.

5.

On the third rung of the City of Brotherly Love,
in an office walled on three sides with erudition,
one with rain, the doctor who held my brother's eleven
holes at birth held a private sitting with my parents

while Tom and I stuck to a sham leather couch. Memory,
like a name-plate, has done the same to a lab coat
the color of empirical truth, a stethoscope clinging
around that expert's neck like the skinniest infant ever

shoved out the window of being. It's pinned itself
to the smell of cleanliness acrid and dense as incense.
Looking down on my parents from this afterlife,
I can see the backs of their heads as clearly as those

of my own hands about to part the past, review
their tragic one-act. They're bracing themselves
in straightbacks, timid to embrace what soon
will be delivered unto them. Today, let my mother

hold out arms by asking the inevitable, about just that,
and let the specialist respond with a cumulative
sentence of silence, a new form of euphemism,
a mincing of words down past the smallest semes

into erasure. Or not euphemism at all, but a statement
flatter, more direct, than any clotted with sound.
And let his muteness, for this woman unlettered in the twists
and contortions of definition, schooled only in loss,

not suffice. Make her press him for something definitive,
press with a lack of patience that borders on, then
crosses the border of impertinence—an attitude
she believes her due, her childbirth right, after all

the suffering she's endured, let loose. About such
human cargoes then, I knew little more than a dimpled
kickball swallowed like a pill by the cancered
widow Brooks's yard, and coughed back flat

a half-week later. I understood whole recesses
kissing nonmetaphoric blades of grass (Scott Spada
my Pandarus), and rain apprehended red-handed
the morning after swiping my three-speed Huffy,

rusty prints all over the gears and chain, but
had yet to crack chaste shell with the egg-tooth
of experience. This time, make it so my mother
requires an estimate she can clutch, like a bed rail,

in the midst of these, her metaphysical labors.
And after the doctor clears his throat, like a cloud
about to publish its dark news, after he lowers lids,
blinding himself that he might see, forbid him

from uttering the shopworn *Time will tell,* as if the clock
kept secrets his downturned lips had not already
let slip. Instead, let her stare him down until he stutters
some occult argot, words so obscure they seem

to withhold half his face, like a surgeon's mask.
Don't let him simply shuffle the latest statistics,
as he did that distant April, inside that balding dome
of his, rub that crystal ball. Whatever you do,

forbid him from drawing a six and calling it the number
of weeks your brother will likely last. You can't view
the fall of another pre-mourning veil, hear the breakage
of your mother's other water, or the depths

of that male voice reading your father's brow, advising
him not to take long trips into self-pity, invest too heavily
in contrition. *It's no one's fault,* he's saying. Can't you
stop him? He's practicing solace like medicine.

Too late. The wall clock's hands have sliced
its own face down the center; the guillotine
of evening has severed Center City from sight.
A late-shifter sweeps past the door, droning

some song of work, one of drudgery's monodies,
and you and Tom are being peeled, fast as Band-Aids,
off Naugahyde, voids made flesh. Forget it now.
We're driving home, silence behind the wheel.

6.

Before going any further, let's get one thing
straight: what precedes and follows is nothing
of the kind. Details, like beads, have been added—
plastic (your call) or pearl—so as not to lose

the thread. To forge is to make and make believe,
develop, and by default, deceive. Really,
can any fact of history be fully seen
or heard, not clogged by sepia-colored wax

or blurred in the 50/50 vision of backward
sight? What's lost in the translation from past
to present is collective gain. You'll need
to remember memory is not merely

an umbrella to be opened against the moment's
jagged slant, but one that perpetually wants
replacing, one we're at a loss from letting slip
from our careless *(weigh the alternative)* grip.

7.

Under the influence once of privilege, I wondered
if it weren't better to live in my brother's state
of vowless chastity, and not be forced to apprentice
in the trade and trade-offs of romantic love,

reface the stuttering teen in memory's rearview
mirror, that knock-kneed, acned four-eyes so shy
he gave his heart (so as not to have it dropped by one
as clumsy as himself) wholly to the unattainable,

beauty that went under the alias Janet Moskowitz—
1976, Haverford Junior High. But then I saw the gift
of limitations one can learn to pronounce laughable,
and it warmed my heart with dread, and I pleaded

for forgiveness, for a world in which romance
would carve my brother's J. S. F. in bark, one in which
he could take a lover, and be taken by one, and feel
the caresses of intimates in darkness losing their minds

to their bodies in making—by their man-and-man-
or man-and-woman-made light—a private transcript
of the eternal dialogue of tension and release, bold
assertion and qualification, recantation and avowal.

More than I want sweet luck to pluck me from this
Tree of Almost-But-Not-Total Ignorance
before an overripe old age, more than I want my voice
to stretch until it breaks a second time, deepens

further, more even than I desire in a cadence
both sloppy and sure to have the first great word
of the century after canto and howl, to fire off one phrase
that strikes the mark so squarely it finds the secret

passage to cliché, I want my brother to get lost
inside the idyllic novella that is an evening of good
conversation, two people making a meal together
of grilled whitefish and Waldorf salad, and later,

of each other. I do believe that when my brother nods
off, the erotic goes on behind his face's closed doors.
But I want him to be able to reach out and touch
(not just with the wishful palps of dream, but with hands

as shapely as those of God and Adam modeled
on Michelangelo's own) another body brimming
with desire, or quickening in the womb of sleep
next to him in bed—in the morning, also, in a steaming

shower. I can see them stepping out without thinking
of slipping, and lightly, between cool tiles and streaming
skylights, kissing, wearing only bathrobes of mist.
I want him to experience lost love, and worse, love

unhad, to sit in the audience of that kind of longing,
that lit but empty stage, and to wake alone after a night
of cheap booze and self-abasement, stand barefoot at the sink
and wait for sunken eyes to rise from the mirror's

murky depths. If only he could make his own decision
whether to vote independent, like me so far, or elect
to marry, start a family, like his brother one rung up.
Tom: the name returns me like "forlorn" to the day after

our mother's voice slit the night, the pair of us in parkas
on the porch, breaths leaving our lips like malformed souls
dissolving over Hefty bags tagged Goodwill, big
with maternity clothes. Inside shone like trust—

she'd polished the hutch and china closet, bureaus
and end tables, stripped off their winter coats of dust.
She'd stooped to brush the black dandruff of flies
from the collars of windowsills, evict the shadows,

level the spiders' vacant tenements. Denial I couldn't
yet confirm had sent forth its shoot. (I don't need
to explain what it's like to deny something undeniable,
and deny you're doing it, right?) Hearing the front door

slam, she rushed and like a supplicant fell
to her knees, spreading arms to hoard us, burying her face
like a plush ax in the rift between our down-filled shoulders.
I remember her first words as hurried, harried

with apology, but what those shards of the fractured
silence were I can't recall, even as I've sensed myself
cut by them many times, sifting through these ruins.
We were kidnap victims ransomed back, but it was she,

prodigal mother, sorrow's spendthrift, who had returned.
I read the score when she withdrew, written in mascara
on the wrinkled staves below her dark, Italian eyes,
the diminutive dirge. It said that something had aged—

her features, my way of seeing them, or both. The smile
she proffered was that of one who'd been through hell
and made it back, and needed to forget there always
exists another hell below the last, some deeper, bedrock

nothingness on which the others get stacked. But
in that smile I first beheld the beauty of repair,
with its stunning frailties, dazzling displays of risk and grace,
each passing hour another step on the ledge of collapse.

8.

For days, she wouldn't let us out of the house,
her sight—kept us on that ocular leash. If it stormed,
she'd haunt Formica, chin on the shelf of one
bent hand, staring at *Days of Our Lives,*

As the World Turns, or out the pantry window,
through her reflection, under the trance of rain.
But by the end of April, the second cruelest month,
the air brightened, started flowing in through screens

not unlike the sieved hatches of whale's throats,
and my mother fell back to the tasks that have fallen
to women like dull harpoons, navigating a steam-iron
in narrow bays of denim and cotton, working the riggings

on which bed sheets dry in the sun. She'd spend hours
at the house's helm, steering spaghetti sauce in circles

84

with the rudder of a wooden spoon, trying to plot
a course that would return us to the Old World—

the world before her final child colonized interiors
she couldn't formerly have conceived, before she met
the cannibal and lost exile huddled within. First outings
to the grocery store produced brown bags sliding down

her arms, full of Hershey's syrup for chocolate milk
and sundaes, maraschino cherries and M&Ms,
Tonka trucks and G. I. Joes, whatever
our untachycardic hearts desired. She simply refused

to refuse. We'd become the spoils of a war we couldn't
fathom or fight. Time, meanwhile, kept dying and being
resurrected, and before long, summer hung on
by a spider's thread in a sycamore down the block.

Before it broke, Rizzo ordered the fire company
to uncork hydrants, defuse the pressures piling up
like horse shit in the streets, and my father got hired
by Quakers to archive precious books. We packed up

and left Spruce and Pine for their signifieds
in the quaint, purgatorial suburbs. Was my mother's face,
once we settled in, still that of a china plate
shattered inside a U-Haul box and epoxied back

together? Was that the September I got glasses and got them
broken, asked how by adults, and didn't rat on foes
I hoped to make friends? Were those the very kids
who learned, as if by magic, of my brother on the other

side of Pennsylvania, who first instructed me in a brand
of imitation that is anything but a form of flattery?
Did they, nonetheless, crowd our welcome mat with gifts
and ersatz smiles on October 5th, to watch a hired clown

wrench balloons into funny shapes, beget a bunny
from a hat, colored hankies from up one sleeve? How's this
for sleights of hand, switcheroos?—my brother Jon
was born on my birth date in Tom's birth month,

and sixteen years from then, to the day, Jessie was born.
God is just, or so some came to believe. Maybe I was one,
but surely now I can't, imagining His great, blundering
hands opening the precious book of my brother's life

and cracking the spine. Like you, I'd give almost anything
to know there exists some resplendent fire in this world
burning so pure and bright we can't help being blind
to it, that in the end, one part of my brother will go

one way, under earth, and another another, that he'll hover
for an evanescent instant between two planes,
one lame foot in this life, one splendid wing in the next.
But surely I can trust that endless flux alone flouts

the abyss, that only the effort of pouring ink, in this
"Song of My Other," up to but not over melodrama's
quivering lip, merits faith, the wringing out of too-sweet
syrup from ragged lines. Those kids returned to our porch

a few weeks later, done up as bloodsuckers, holey
specters, bandaged (like our dogwood after Mischief
Night) mummies. They took Mallow Cups, miniature
Snickers, and me, the hobo, with them. Surely, I am

sure of none of this. Another few weeks, and my father
rose, half drunk on table wine, half on togetherness,
and lifted his glass and voice to offer some lovable,
secular thanks. Neighbors' chimneys started dreaming,

and then the first flake fell, bringing down autumn
with it. Before the last, the southeast corner of the state
keeping our nuclear family extended was blotted out.
The smeared *Main Line Times* reported a record

twenty inches, that a car's rear bumper had bitten
off the mitten and middle finger of a Radnor teen.
Jesus got born, then the hour of the Great Antitheses:
Watergate and disco. One Sunday we drove

to watch the long barge of ice sail the Schuykill
before spring sank it. By Valentine's, I'd fallen for
Mrs. Freilich, SRA books, and behind in math, frustrated
with fractions and divisions, rhomboids and other odd shapes.

Suzanne Munsel passed chicken pox around
class like a rumor of how babies are made,
and my tongue and a tasteless wafer got united.
Pisces swam into view and the moon filled out,

as my father promised soon my slight frame would—
oh, soon. It floated on top of the sky, like a bobber,
then plunged, and March 5th set its hook a second time.
Trying not to with all her might, my mother hauled up

the day from depths she'd stopped studying
in therapy's one-room schoolhouse. She screwed up
her lips and began to wrestle with a math of her own,
the incalculable fact that she'd let the subtraction

of one increase the value of the other two,
that the equilateral triangle of sons she'd dreamed
of drawing had come out isosceles. A new grimace
made it seem as if, in recrimination, she'd stuck

herself with that sharp shape, its hilt protruding
from her side like a phantom limb. She locked her voice
in its tight box, gulped the key, and descended into her
upperworld again, impregnating the bed whose mattress

had memorized the contours of her depression.
A fresh morning sickness stretched into afternoons,

evenings, and I knew among the forsythia's pre-fireworks
that my brother's twin had begun to swell inside her,

the dark child she has yet to wean from herself.
My mother won't declare it, but I think the Catholic
schoolgirl she still carries beneath her skin, like a benign
cyst, believes, at some point, she must have committed

unforgivable sins that made my brother's toes
embody ten commandments disobeyed. I don't know
if she'll ever forgive herself for bringing him
into the world disfigured, into the fold of history

and circumstance to bleat with the rest of us
brave sheep, cowardly lions. I do know it's unpragmatic
to attempt to count how often I've pondered her choice
whether or not to raise him, how frequently I've thought

of those towers on either side—fate's hatchetmen.
Daughter of Levi, who bore a son and hid her eyes,
daughter of Pharaoh, who drew an ungodly child
from the waters of herself, yet never drew his body

to her own (never felt that last contraction), woman
of two minds over a boy scarcely with one, I feel for you
as I do all those raised to praise perfection,
to put undying faith in unadulterated gods. To honor

something deeply, your son has taught me,
is to love what's hapless, vulnerable in it. Prize
the world's caprice, is his slurred sermon, worship
that. We must learn to cherish chance to have one.

9.

What's memorable is cheap detail, as if triviality itself
were the handful of change that must be tossed
before the gate to past lives lifts. I think I might
survive on scraps thrown to myself of that trip

across the state which had come between our family
like a silly argument no one will fess up to starting.
The hatchback Vega, that sizzling tip of a 311-mile fuse,
long ago fizzled to rust; the distance that appeared to go

up in immaculate flames, has, for good. Still, I bank
on a ramp in Conshohocken, as if this fly's-eye view
could be conflated to a single lens, one hand-held
glass to magnify, detect the lost. I reclaim Go Fish,

doodles in a cosmos-covered composition book,
rows of feed-corn shuffled by speed, fellow pilgrims—
Alfa—stacked like solitaire at tolls, my mother dividing
the cramped back seat like a PBJ, then burying herself

in murder, getting six chapters under by Harrisburg.
I can't forget having to go (taboo to ask my father
to pull to the side) in a Folger's can—*Bonneville*—
Tom and I sniggering uncontrollably at Gap,

Intercourse, Paradise on the map, the tiresome climb
to the peak of boredom (that nadir), the stench of diesel
and no time passing. Man's best friend lay roadside,
remember? eulogized—*Corvair*—by a pair of crows,

the sky's blue arm, as though in consolation, draped
over the shoulders of hills my father cursed, trying
to tune in "Your Cheating *(Dodge Dart!)* Heart."
Double points! I quit. You lose. I said, I quit. Cut it . . .

static, static . . . *out. His fault. Nuntuhh. Uhuh.*
Quiet! Asphalt, asphalt, asphalt. East, east,
sliding off quarter-panels, fenders, white lines running
like a spine down the turnpike's back. There was,

I'm convinced, a young guy kneeling as if to propose
to lug nuts, our better luck whizzing past, its catlike
neeeoww a kind of ridicule, and not long later, the music
of infinitesimal spheres on the tinny roof, the twin

metronome of wipers slap-slapping lullaby time.
The scene ahead grew fuzzy then with flashing
reds and blues. Traffic slowed, crawled past the twisted
corpse of a retread, tiny ice cubes of glass, a jackknifed

eighteen-wheeler, contorted Malibu (no points),
fluorescent triangles standing guard. A woman sat
wrapped in wool, faint drizzle, hugging herself—
shivering, I surmise today, from having veered

so close to frigidity and survived with hardly a scratch,
the memory of impact alone coating her eyes.
My mother rubbernecked around her bucket seat—
Lot's wife—froze on wreckage for a moment, then

returned to safer investigations, the dandy Poirot.
What to do but follow? I found my dog-ear,
Huck being chased in circles around the cabin,
Pap sauced on whiskey, flailing "with a clasp-knife,"

calling his boy the "Angel of Death." Minutes later,
my stomach started turning with them. Out of my
allotment of glass I peered, trees speeding past speeding
the nausea. Something like transgression began

to climb my throat: *Dad . . .*   *I know,* he said,
and somehow did—arced to the shoulder, jerked
the hand brake, thrust open his door and hefted
the lid off a billowing pot. Providence is a Vega

vomiting first. Hours later, AAA dropped us off
at Howard Johnson's. Huck and Jim had drifted past
St. Louis, boarded a steamboat suicidal on stormy
rocks, listened in on murderers, lost their raft.

I'd learned *GM couldn't make a decent water pump*
if the nation's fate relied on it. My father steered himself
to a bar across the street, to spend time with his other
family, while my mother signed the registration slip

with a sigh as long as her name. Was it before
or after clam strips, fries and malts, was the sun
above or burrowed under the Tuscaroras, when Lot
rapped on the door at last with puckish knuckles?

My mother didn't move, kept her focus locked
on Petrocelli working the courtroom, inserting key
pieces of truth sure to send some lowlife up the river.
The next was no knock, and I leaped up, twisted

the knob. He burst in howling, doubled over,
spanking his knee. Had the TV attorney's quarry
confessed, pronounced his sentence of remorse,
before my father (after registering the room's total

dearth of amusement) wiped giddiness from lips
that became a long dash followed by no explanation?
I do recall him, with a grumble, switching off the set,
ending the day with the white period at the center

of its screen. Next morning, at buzz of six, he nudged
my shoulder, said get dressed, keeping, as if in shame,
his eyes receded (though I did glimpse the Doppler
effect they'd undergone overnight). Tommy was

lowered dozing, gently in the back, the way our mother
always treated the one grocery bag cradling eggs.
Then the shifter got torqued to D, the pedal punched.
Tires squealed like a struck pup, and soon the Vega

whimpered on all four cylinders, its chassis quaking
to the bolts, hurtling past 50, 60, the needle fearful,
pistons tapping, 70, like yesterday's rain. *David, you'll
get us killed!* But he was oblivious, bullying back time.

10.

As if nature had learned the trick of prefiguration,
my feet, at two, pigeoned in so far I'd take a step,

they say, then another, and topple like a Legos tower.
For eighteen months, my lower half was cast in plaster.

For eighteen years, my brother traveled home
for Christmas via envelope. The card and Polaroid
would make the rounds at supper, and each would take
a helping of the little good another year had done him,

the cheery report of progress we knew was powdered
cookies and sugarplums, finger cakes frosted
with a nun's best cursive, though none could
resist those sweets. Of the few photos I know survive,

one captures him in the lobby trimmed with spruce
and crèche, papier-mâché apostles, shiny presents,
other holy tinsel. He's happy, maybe eight, *and standing,*
the metal scaffolding of restoration about his legs.

The floor gleams like ice that likely skinned the ponds
outside Pittsburgh the day the shot got snapped
like a frozen twig beneath another kid's wet boot.
I stared long, the afternoon it came, into the glossy

pane, made reprints in my mind all night.
It was after two, I think, when I exposed the scam
scrawled in shadow on one of its celluloid walls.
See that figure barely standing outside the frame?

She's poised to catch my brother if he falls between
Smile, and the shutter's swift chomp out of time.
Can you picture this woman in her habit dashing
to K-Mart, prancing up and down the aisles,

returning with a sack of film to calm families
from Cincinnati to Scranton? Maybe then you can
comprehend why I blinked back sleep till daybreak,
giving the remains of faith I might have harbored

their last rites; why I cursed all those who must
have seen in my brother's suffering something
of their Lord's, who no doubt whispered in his ear
that he'd be given wings someday, as long as

he earned them with the inverse bombing missions
of prayer. Well, I was sixteen, fiery-tempered, strung
out on pot and Blake, wielding a tongue double-edged
with sarcasm and contempt, trying, I see now,

to forge a new life with which to slay the old.
Today, I suppose I recognize my debt to those
whose firm convictions did overthrow the Greek
rejection of human ruin. But I'd be lying

if I said the shadow in that photo doesn't haunt me,
that sterile hall. At least twice I walked it—first
to the office where a superior mother hid her left hand
with her right, and spoke to my parents in nurturing,

condescending tones, sensing, it appeared, what they
had become: two children cowering under the punishing
gaze of their own botched parenting. I knew, even then,
her words were motel soap, filched shampoo in impish bottles,

wouldn't last long after that trip. The second was alone,
after being granted permission to get a sip of water
at the porcelain fountain. In the waiting room
where I killed a half an hour, I read that my Phils

were slated to face the Bucs that night.
I wanted to watch my heroes, Greg Luzinski
and Bobby Tolan, round the bases, rack up run after run,
knock holes in the sky with strokes of physical genius,

but knew it was out of the question. The only diamond
I'd see was a glistening shard of spittle in the corner
of my brother's mouth, as he lay in a side-barred bed,
clueless who we were. Still, I kept dreaming on

the infernal trip home (that destination we hoped
to reach all along) of rooting for my squad
in the hostile waters of Pittsburgh's famed Three Rivers.
Those fictive cheers return me now to real,

fireworks just soaring off the ground.
With hands clapped over her ears, Jessie
flinches in ecstasy, unable to believe her eyes.
Our family is gathered under families of stars,

ungraspable sparklers, and from this hill, gazing
down on the lower constellations of the city,
every one of us is oohing and aahing. We've had to
drop my brother at his apartment, batteries

run totally down. The air has cooled a bit,
no longer smells of grilling meat, and the trees
are having epiphanies in the open. Giant dice
just rumbled overhead, but it won't dare

rain—not before this voluminous light show
ends, or the last of these ten musings
fizzles to a close. Here comes the finale now,
a crescendo of popping whites, reds and blues.

My semi-patriotic heart flutters, a moth
at their flames. I wonder if my brother's asleep
already, or whether, drowsily, he hears
these explosions in the distance as dull applause.

Selected by Robert Fink, *Strange Pietà* is the twelfth winner of the Walt McDonald First-Book Competition in Poetry. The Competition is supported generously through donated subscriptions from *The American Scholar, The Atlantic Monthly, The Georgia Review, Gulf Coast, The Hudson Review, The Massachusetts Review, Poetry, Shenandoah,* and *The Southern Review.*

Gregory Fraser won the David Austen Award for best poetry manuscript, judged by Stanley Kunitz, at Columbia University. Also a winner of the Donald Barthelme Prize and the James Michener Award for Poetry, Gregory Fraser teaches literature and creative writing at the State University of West Georgia, outside Atlanta. *Strange Pietà* is a two-time finalist for the Walt Whitman Award from the Academy of American Poets.